The Pivot Point:

 *SUCCESS IN ORGANIZATIONAL CHANGE*

The Pivot Point:

>>> *SUCCESS IN*
ORGANIZATIONAL CHANGE

Dr. Victoria M. Grady
Dr. James D. Grady

NEW YORK

LONDON • NASHVILLE • MELBOURNE • VANCOUVER

The Pivot Point:

SUCCESS IN ORGANIZATIONAL CHANGE

Published in New York, New York, by Morgan James Publishing. Morgan James is a trademark of Morgan James, LLC. www.MorganJamesPublishing.com

ISBN 9781614483007 paperback
ISBN 9781614483014 eBook
Library of Congress Control Number: 2012936897

Cover Design by:
Rachel Lopez www.r2cdesign.com

Interior Design by:
Bonnie Bushman bonnie@caboodlegraphics.com

Morgan James is a proud partner of Habitat for Humanity Peninsula and Greater Williamsburg. Partners in building since 2006.

Get involved today! Visit
MorganJamesPublishing.com/giving-back

In Memory of

David Joseph Goetz
(1969-2003)

Table of Contents

"We believe that 'resistance to change' isn't about resistance at all."

Introduction

There's an unsolved mystery *in your company. Will you be the one to solve it?*

Everyone in your office has been acting strange lately. Normally patient co-workers are storming off in a huff. Normally quiet co-workers are having meltdowns over the most insignificant issues. Why this is happening really isn't a mystery: you're pretty sure it has to do with all the change that's been happening at work. Whether in your leadership, your business processes, your software, or your staffing, change has become the new constant for your organization, and quite frankly, it's not getting any easier. You've heard that the board has approved yet another set of large-scale changes that are supposed to make your company even "leaner," but they don't yet know how lean it's going to get; you're still trying to replace staff from the flurry of resignations that came from the last round of revamped processes.

You thought you had done everything right. You had hired experienced change consultants and had followed all of their recommended steps: creating a sense of urgency, communicating explanations and information, generating a vision, creating leadership teams, and integrating all the right steps in the right order. Yet the general mood of the organization had worsened, and implementation was lagging far behind schedule. And that's when the resignations began. What went wrong? What are you missing?

But here's a bigger problem; even though this kind of upheaval is commonplace for any given change initiative in almost any organization, most organizational change experts still don't fully understand why either. It's not for lack of trying. Precisely because change has become the new constant, gifted and well-intentioned thinkers and practitioners have applied their best efforts to help organizations understand and manage organizational change. In fact, research in the discipline of organizational change management has exploded over the past fifteen years or so, and new research-based and undeniably logical models promising successful organizational change are emerging all the time. But despite all these advances in the field, *the vast majority of organizational change initiatives still fail.* In fact, the failure rate averaged 68 percent for the fifteen years prior to Standish (2009), and 71% in the five years before Standish (2015). You're not the only one who's missing something.

Many experts believe they've discovered at least one of the reasons behind this stubborn failure rate; "employee resistance to change." They believe many organizational problems in general, and the failure of organizational change initiatives in particular, can be blamed on this "resistance." Here's how some have characterized it:

> Left unattended, the impacts of [resistance to] change reduce employee and organizational productivity,

contribute to burnout, negatively impact the quality of products and services, damage customer relations, and reduce employee morale (Bennett 2001).

According to Mark Tannenbaum of QED in Washington, DC, "Depending on the nature of the workplace and the latitude to address personnel issues, resistance among employees can foster negativity, skepticism, and low morale, and, consequently, lower productivity. These behaviors can be far-reaching, resulting in the loss of the most productive workers, the 'trenching-in' mentality of the least productive, and the incalculable costs to the financial, personnel, customer loyalty, reputation to the organization" (Bennett 2001).

[E]mployee resistance is pervasive in organizational change. Resistance is often a natural response to change and is expected to take place particularly when employees feel: (a) that change is out of their control, (b) pressured to change without feeling valued, (c) distrust toward the organization, and (d) that they are seen by the organization simply as resources towards change (Celnar 1999).

Whether the company is a Fortune 100 colossus or a modest not-for-profit, a family business, or a professional organization, the problem is that people fear change, resist it, fight it, and often end up sabotaging what they might even consciously agree are good means to move things forward... (Eisold 2010).

Yet even after identifying the problem as "employee resistance to change," not one organizational change model has been able to prevent it, or consistently reduce its negative impact on the organization.

There is an unsolved mystery in the field of organizational change, and the experts seem to have reached a dead end. The next step should not be just to keep doing the same thing we've been doing, nor should we simply call it a cold case and give up.

It's time to take matters into your own hands and think like a detective. How do detectives solve difficult crimes, the ones with no obvious motive or evidence? First, they have a *driving passion* to solve the problem. Their motivation compels them to look in unlikely, faraway places for any clue that might help them put the puzzle together correctly. Second, they understand how their *assumptions and biases* can close their minds to clues that might be hidden in plain sight. They don't dismiss any possible evidence that could be connected, just because no one's ever connected it before. Third, they base their theories on *hard evidence*; those puzzle pieces might appear to be different colors, but until they actually put them together to see if they fit, they won't know for sure, will they?

If that lead turns into a dead end, that's where their driving passion to solve the mystery comes in; they'll move on to the next lead and start the process all over again. The best detectives use all three of these qualities simultaneously, and most of all, they have an unshakable faith that there *is* an answer that makes sense of all the facts. They just haven't looked hard enough yet.

We don't doubt the passion or the logical abilities of the organizational change experts in solving the mystery of this persistently high change failure rate. But we do wonder if perhaps their *assumptions* keep them looking for clues in the same well-lit but empty room. What if this is not a "resistance" problem for which the organization must engineer a solution, but a deeper "people" problem that the organization must first learn to understand and respect?

For example, if we say someone "resists" something, we're implying they're consciously and actively doing so. We certainly admit that employees' actions, as a result of change initiatives, can disrupt the entire organization. But that doesn't mean they're consciously "resisting" change. The question is, *why* do employees, either knowingly or unknowingly, have such difficulty with change? And more importantly, what can be done to help them adjust?

Fifteen years ago, during my (VMG's) masters' degree graduate studies, I was employed as a senior manager in the software training industry. On a daily basis, I found myself perplexed by the intensely emotional response of individual employees from all types of organizations when new technology was introduced. Later in my career, I witnessed a similar reaction from individual employees impacted by change in management, leadership, and business processes as well. People were reacting emotionally to change in almost any organizational context, but I could find no thread to understand the connection. To begin my investigation, I started taking notes and putting them in a folder under this title: "Notes on common responses in individuals to different types of organizational change and the difficulties these responses present."

These notes ended up spanning six years and two continents, with observations from the southern United States, the eastern and northeastern United States, and central and southern Germany. I recorded my conversations with exasperated employees in geographically, demographically, and culturally distinct areas, and their reaction to change in technology, business processes, leadership, physical location, and structure. They all inadvertently identified an intense internal struggle in dealing with change. It wasn't that these individual employees were not good at change, or that they hated change, or that they were resistant to change, it was as if they were all dealing with an *internal* struggle that seemed inherent to the process of adjusting to change. And this internal struggle was not responding to external solutions.

But Why?

In 2001, I gained some additional insight into the answer, as I found myself sitting in an Individual and Group Dynamics course at The George Washington University. Dr. Jerry B. Harvey was presenting a new concept he termed the "anaclitic depression blues," and he was in full control of my attention. His topic came from a chapter in his recently published book, *How Come Every Time I Get Stabbed in the Back My Fingerprints Are on the Knife?*, that discussed the emotional responses of employees during periods of organizational downsizing.

At some moment during that lecture I was hit by a lightning bolt, and I blurted out, "You're saying that this emotional response relates to the nature of the change employees experience during a layoff. Interestingly, I have been listening to employees dealing with technology change, organizational structure change, leadership change, reporting-status change, and process change since 1995, and they were all dealing with this 'blues' thing, too!"

Catching myself as I became aware of the abruptness of my interruption, I changed the tone of my voice. "Is it possible this type of depression is related to *all* types of change … that it is really not just a resistance to the change, but so much deeper than that?"

His gaze was fixed on me with a probing intensity, but after that prolonged moment of uncharacteristic silence, Dr. Harvey calmly responded, "Perhaps you have found a topic for your dissertation, Ms. Grady, and not only that, considering the intensity of your apparent convictions, perhaps you have found a lifelong research path as well."

This book is about the passionate drive to solve the mystery of a troubling problem by searching "outside the box." If we keep looking in the same brightly lit room for clues, the only thing we'll find is a lot of frustration, and perhaps a temptation to blame the victim. So our first task is to discard our assumptions and think like a detective. To find relevant clues, we may have to search in dark alleyways and be willing to visit unfamiliar places, including fields of study outside organizational change theory—and maybe even outside business itself.

The first part of this book is a "story" about how one persistent consultant discovered key evidence in the mystery of the frustrating failure rate for organizational change initiatives in an unlikely place. Is this newly discovered evidence relevant? Is Dr. Harvey's theory convincing? To solve the mystery, we need to think like a detective and render an informed verdict. In the section that follows the story, we'll lay out all the science behind his theory so you can examine the very same information as he and his team did.

We'll admit our bias from the beginning; we are convinced by the evidence. Once we were able to discard our assumptions that this is purely an organizational problem with a purely organizational solution, or that difficult employees are to blame for the problem, a bigger picture started to take shape.

We believe that "resistance to change" isn't about resistance at all. The difficulty employees have with change is instead a natural response that is grounded in human nature and provides us with a hard-wired biological instinct, not an empty excuse, for a reaction that is as common as change itself. This evidence will support the organizations' effort to achieve the "pivot point" of success in change initiatives. In this book, *The Pivot Point,* we will introduce these concepts.

But don't let our verdict influence yours. To solve this mystery, you need to think like a detective. Read the story. Examine the science. Conduct your own investigation in your organization. You be the judge.

The Story: Looking Beyond Resistance

I t was a dark and stormy Saturday night in Washington, DC, and it was growing darker. The conference at a hotel in the Chinatown district had been canceled, but not everyone could make it out before the hurricane hit. The hotel staff and a few family members were huddled together in a remote corner of the lobby, where faces were lit sporadically by flashing lightning. A few of the remaining conference participants were gathered in a nearby conference room, with quiet conversations starting and then trailing off, unfinished. The hurricane wasn't the only thing on their minds.

Suddenly, a deafening crash of lightning illuminated the tall windows, and they heard a sickening crack. Everything went black. Someone screamed. Then one of the hotel staff stood up and called, "Marie? Marie, where are you?" His four-year-old daughter was nowhere to be found. The small group of guests and staff split up and began searching blindly in the lobby and connecting dark corridors. A half hour later, the girl had still not been found. "What if she went outside?" her father said, in a panic. Pulling his keys from his pocket, he started to unlock the door leading to the patio, when he saw two flashlight beams bobbing toward him in the darkness and heard a voice call out: "We found her—don't worry, she's just fine, " it said, clearly holding something back. "Just come with us, you really need to see this!

> > > > >

Just a few days earlier, the weather was clear and spirits were high. The first conference of the International Society for the Study of Organizational Management (ISSOM) had begun Wednesday evening with great fanfare and excitement. Based on the conversations at the reception that night, it was evident they were drawing many of the best and the brightest from second- and third-tier management. Sponsored and coordinated by a distinguished group of business, industry, and government organizations representing seven countries, ISSOM's membership process was stringent; employers had to first nominate prospective members, and then nominees' credentials were further scrutinized before the committee issued the invitation to join. The conference organizers were also delighted to notice the wide variety of organizations that were represented. The conference theme was "Management, Leadership and Change in the Global Economy". With the breadth of expertise represented here, it promised to be a productive event that could establish a strong reputation for the organization.

The conference would run from Wednesday evening to Sunday at noon. So far it had been running fairly smoothly, with participants engaging energetically with each other between sessions. But on Friday morning, a hurricane in the Atlantic took a sharp turn towards the east coast of the United States, with its most likely path centering on Washington, DC. By Friday noon, the hurricane was projected to strengthen further, and enter the metropolitan area on Saturday evening with a vengeance. Greatly disappointed, the conference planners resigned themselves to cancelling the rest of the conference. That afternoon, they announced that the conference would officially and prematurely end after the last speaker of the day. Participants rushed to change their travel plans.

By the time the last speaker took the stage later Friday afternoon, only half of the participants were left. But despite the distractions, the speaker, Dr. William Bankston electrified his audience with an informative presentation titled "Mystery on the Organizational Express." His presentation was as full of unanswered questions as it was of candor, spontaneity, and a dry sense of humor as big as his home state of Texas. Unfortunately, this just made the premature conclusion of the conference feel all the more unfinished, as its potential value was waved like a white flag once more before the audience. The breakout group sessions with the afternoon's speakers that were to follow had been cancelled. The remaining conference attendees prepared for departure.

> > > > >

"Hey, Edward," a young man shouted over his shoulder, luggage in hand, as he was walking through the front door in the hotel lobby, "I'll see you next week at Harry's, okay? Be smart and stay safe."

A tall, rather thin, man, with unkempt blond hair, self-consciously stepped away from the group he was with and shouted back, "Just don't send me one of those 'wish you were here' messages after you get back to England tomorrow!" He noticed as he turned back to the group that one or two had been startled by the volume of his voice—he had been a bit startled by it himself. Sheepishly, he explained in lower tones, "He lives in a neighborhood near me. I think he got the last ticket home." Under his breath, he added, "He's always been a lucky *&#!"

The conference registrar was conferring with another group of sponsors and speakers who were also startled at the outburst. After another moment, the registrar left his group and walked up to the other group, consisting mostly of anxious attendees who, like Edward, still hadn't finalized their travel plans. "I hope you understand that we have done all we can to get you out of here in a timely fashion," said the registrar apologetically. "Still, even though you were unable to reschedule your departure for today, I trust that you will all be able to leave before they close the airport tomorrow afternoon."

One man, an African American wearing a dark brown suit and a tan knit shirt, spoke up. "Well, it seems most of us will be able to get out, but there are a few who couldn't reschedule their travel plans and have to wait until Sunday—that is, if the hurricane will let them."

"Wait here just a moment," the registrar said, and he walked back over to the group of speakers and sponsors, getting ready to leave. After a brief discussion, all shook hands and dispersed—except for that day's last speaker, Dr. Bankston, who was now standing alone, holding a stack of folders.

Dr. Bankston walked over to the group, smiling enigmatically. "So, I hear y'all are stranded too, for the time being. How about you join me for breakfast tomorrow morning, here at the hotel?"

A sudden crash of thunder resounded throughout the lobby—nothing could have provided a better punctuation mark for the astonished looks on the faces of those in the group at that instant. But one by one, they responded, "Sure." "Yes, I can do that." "Why, thank you; that would be fine."

Dr. Bankston nodded in approval and headed toward the elevator, leaving the remaining participants wondering about the nature of this unexpected meeting.

Saturday Morning—7:56 a.m.

The next morning, a young woman dressed in a dark gray suit and discreetly ruffled blue blouse was the first to arrive in the lobby. Almost as soon as she stepped out of the elevator, a hotel employee from guest services, holding a bag, greeted her. "One of Dr. Bankston's guests?" she asked pleasantly. "Yes, I am," she replied, a little uncertain. "I'm Joan."

The woman did not identify herself by name, but replied, "You'll be dining in the courtyard this morning—follow me, please." Joan followed her outside where the air was heavy with impending rain. But the chorus of natural sounds and the clatter of dishes were a welcome change from the suddenly silent hotel.

The lady from guest services gestured to a table, and as Joan sat down, she opened the bag and began distributing small gift boxes, wrapped with a blue ribbon, at each place setting. "Your host asked me to make sure each of you got one of these," she said, smiling again. After she had placed the final one at the head of the table, she said, "Enjoy your breakfast," and returned to the lobby.

One by one the other guests arrived, guided by the same guest services representative. Soon most of the sixteen chairs around the patio tables were filled, with the one at the head conspicuously vacant. "I wonder what these are—tickets home?" joked a woman with vaguely Asian features, picking up the gift box on her plate. Joan forgot—she was the only one who had seen the hotel employee distribute these packages. "Oh, of course. A woman from guest services gave these out— she said they were from Dr. Bankston. I was assuming he'd be here himself to explain them."

As if on cue, they heard footsteps and a brief conversation outside the door. Dr. Bankston walked out onto the patio with a bit of a flourish and then said, "Oh, good, you're already here. Let's get started, shall we?" It was 8:00 a.m.

Dr. Bankston's reputation in the field of management was legendary. Even if the attendees hadn't seen his presentation yesterday, they would have known that he was both a respected educator and a well-known consultant in high demand in business and industry. He was known as idiosyncratic, tireless, and obsessive (if unconventional) in his pursuit of solving the "unsolved mysteries" of past, current, and future management theory. He seemed to have mastered the art of being just enough in control to be feared, and just approachable enough to be revered. In truth, he had volunteered to personally work with the stranded conference participants—not just because he was stranded too, but because he felt there was still some unfinished business introduced but not resolved by the conference sessions.

He said to the group, "I have in my hand a folder with receipts for all the prepaid hotel services, which includes food and lodging. The lodging was for yesterday's and today's speakers, and the food services include last night's cancelled reception and tonight's cancelled dinner banquet.

Considering it is all prepaid and these payments are not refundable, we have the challenge of meeting, eating, and lodging to our heart's content. I surmise some of you will be leaving for the airport shortly, so consider this your *bon voyage* breakfast, and best wishes for an uneventful trip home. For those of us left stranded, I say we eat, drink, and be merry, at least until tomorrow afternoon when all of the vouchers will become invalid. Perhaps in the meantime, if we can shed a ray of light or two on the "mystery" I discussed yesterday, so much the better.

"Oh," he said as an afterthought, "as for the little packages—as a favor to me, please keep them with you. They each possess a charm to ward off the ill effects of the hurricane. But don't open them, or the charm will surely escape."

He stood, and then with an exaggerated wave of his hand, several servers paraded out onto the patio with tray after tray of breakfast food. "I've always wanted to do that," he said with a chuckle. "After we eat, let's break for an hour. Several of you will still need to get to the airport this morning; if you are already packed, then there is plenty of time for you to have a bite to eat. While you are here, and if you will pardon me if I speak with my mouth full, I will try to answer as many of your questions as possible. I'm told the van will be out front by the time you finish. For those of you who, like me, are here for the duration, I'll be back in the conference room at about 10:00 a.m., that is, if any of you are interested in contemplating a management topic of great significance."

He glanced around at the business attire of his guests. "One suggestion: casual is the dress of the day—hell, I didn't bring anything comfortable myself, so I may just wear my pajamas," he chuckled. "We will begin with the establishment of an agenda when we return. I think determining mealtimes," he said, as he finished off a pastry, "should be the first order of business, don't you agree?"

There was much food consumed and no small amount of nervous energy expended as the clouds got lower and more menacing over the patio. Conversations were mostly superficial and storm focused, quite unlike the conversations Dr. Bankston had overheard over the past few days. The story was always the same; organizations had a sense of a haunting restlessness that was perhaps similar to the restlessness in the assembled group due to the approaching hurricane. Much of the time the lower-level employees were distracted and unaware of the danger signs, or, if aware, they had chosen to ignore the signs. Many of those who were in decision-making positions were at least vaguely aware of the problems, but had no clue as to the origin.

The general sense of organizational melancholy, happening in different parts of the organization and in different parts of the globe, is too consistent to just be coincidental, Dr. Bankston had thought. *There must be some common thread that connects these seemingly unrelated problems.* The detective in him was already at work.

Finally the last few stragglers finished eating, politely offered their thanks, and those with planes to catch headed straight to the waiting airport shuttle.

Dr. Bankston leaned back in his chair, surveying the empty table. Then he sat up, drained his coffee cup, wiped his mouth one last time, and stood up. He had some time to kill before ten o'clock.

> "There must be some common thread that connects these seemingly unrelated problems."

He had been particularly troubled by the unrest in the organizational world, but for the first time in several days, as he wandered around isolated corridors, his thoughts shifted to the growing feeling of unrest inside himself. He had first noticed it several years ago. Old age, he had decided, and looked no further—until recently. It re-emerged three months ago, about the time his home computer had crashed. It was an old friend of many years, helping him produce scores of presentations and papers, and two—nearly three—books. His computer had seemingly developed a persona, and he had even given it a name: "Betsy." But all of a sudden, Betsy had died, right in the middle of writing his third book, which still remained unfinished. For some reason he thought back to that moment in time when he first noticed a lingering sense of annoyance—he had even felt anxious in his little home office. Although it was just a small corner of the basement, it had always been for him a sanctuary. He was not particularly superstitious, but ... if only that damned computer had not died. No, that was silly; its replacement was much faster and more capable than Betsy...

He refocused his attention. *Now, getting back to the real problem at hand: what is going on in the organizational world? How can I work with this group in order to get a better impression of the problems they confront? Where can I gain some insight into this mystery?* As he was lost in thought, he almost stumbled into one of the participants. Somehow he had found his way back to the door to the conference room. "Excuse me," he said apologetically. "I was lost in thought."

"Me too, Dr. Bankston; sorry for not watching where I was going. My name is Hilde," she said with a slight German accent and added, as a crimson blush enveloped her neck, "and I really do appreciate your willingness to share time with us."

"My pleasure, Hilde—nice to meet you. Shall we go in?"

The Introductions—10:00 a.m.

Following Hilde, Dr. Bankston entered the room with purpose and took his seat at the head of the table. "Well, it seems that I have run most of you off," he stated energetically. Out of the fourteen participants that showed up for breakfast, it appeared ten had departed for the airport. "But this size is really better. Why don't we begin with introductions and—uh-oh, looks like we have a late arrival—well, sit down and join the crew. I was saying ... how about each of you tell us a little about yourself and your organization?

"But before you begin your introductions, let me first be honest with you. I am troubled by what I have overheard at this conference over the past few days, which also reflects what I've seen in my own recent work. Apparently storm clouds are gathering over business and industry, and no one seems to know how to determine the source of the problem. I guess hurricanes are easier to figure out than "organizational storms".

"The truth is, shedding some light on this mystery has become a preoccupation of mine, and I hope you can help me gain some insight into the situation. So to the extent you are comfortable sharing your feelings and insights, please be as honest as you can with yourself and with us. It will be helpful if you tell us about some of the challenges that you are personally confronting at work, and also about the challenges faced by your organization in general. Also, if you will, please include in your comments your personal vision and your vision for your organization. I'm looking for clues that may lead us to some answers.

"Who wants to start us off? You there, late arrival, I saw you speaking for others in the group last night. Will you go first?" he said, gesturing toward the man, dressed in a button-down and khakis, who had just found a seat.

"Me? Well, okay," he replied. He started to stand, then thought better of it, and began. "Okay. My name is Jake, and I am Deputy Director for Consumer Information at a federal government agency headquartered here in the Washington, DC area. I manage a system for disseminating information to consumers regarding applications and policies as they relate to our areas of responsibility. Before that, I was a marketing director for a banking home office in the Baltimore area, with about 120 employees spread over seven locations. I left the bank for my present position because of the federal government benefits and retirement plan. I have a master's degree in public relations and have been in my present position for over four years. My talents seem to favor interpersonal communication and the ability to empathize with the underdog.

JAKE

Jake is a forty-two-year-old African American who grew up in a lower-middle-class suburb between Baltimore and Washington, DC. He was married for a short while after graduating from high school. He and his wife had no children, and they divorced after less than a year. He then joined the US Air Force, where he served for an uneventful four years. He used the GI Bill to attend a large university in Maryland, and after receiving a degree in marketing, he worked in banking for twelve years in the Silver Springs area near where he grew up.

During the early years after his return, he cared for his ailing mother and eventually purchased a small townhouse nearer Washington. After her death, he attended George Mason University and received a master's degree in Public Administration. He accepted a mid-level managerial position four years ago with a federal government agency and received two substantial promotions during that short period of time. He is now Deputy Director for Consumer Information for his division and is presently being considered for promotion to a position of considerably more influence.

Personality: He is warm-hearted, conscientious, and strives to achieve harmony. He is primarily interested in those things that directly or indirectly improve the quality of life for others.

"My challenge at work is that I want to make everyone happy, an impossible task—and that I tend to take those problems home with me, which is probably one of the reasons I am single at the moment. The organizational challenge that I deal with is that my employees tend to take the opposite approach—they are short tempered, they don't communicate well, and they rarely ever empathize with respondents. Most employees just seem committed to their paychecks and the weekend. It is as if they have been battered and bruised into not caring. Most of them are basically good people, but for reasons I do not understand, they seem to be distracted much of the time.

"Dr. Bankston, you said we should be honest with each other, so I guess I will be—I mentioned that I live here in the DC area. I could have easily gone back to my condo, but I would really like to participate in these sessions. I don't know why; I just have an intuition this will be a productive twenty-four hours."

There was some mock applause.

"Well, Jake, I hope your 'intuition' is right. Who can beat that? Anyone want to go next?"

The woman who had joked about the gift boxes at breakfast said, "No, I won't even try to beat that, but I will go next, because I agree with Jake's intuition and feel I have the opportunity to benefit, too. So, on with the show. My name is Elizabeth, but I prefer Liz. I'm married with two nearly grown children, and I am a physician. In that capacity I serve as VP and medical director at a community hospital in the Midwest. This is the only hospital serving an area of about 380,000 people. We are progressive in our approach to patient care, and we are a bit ahead of the curve compared to other hospitals in the state, but that means our expenses are a little higher, and that presents another challenge.

LIZ

Liz, forty-four, is the oldest daughter of a marriage between a Korean-American mother and an American father. Her parents had met and married when her father was on assignment to the US embassy in South Korea. She was born shortly after her parents arrived back in the States, and because of her father's frequent travels and her mother's shyness, she developed a confident and independent personality and was able to handle many of the family's matters at an early age.

After graduation from high school and college, she attended a private medical school in California, where she graduated with honors. She specialized in family practice and returned to practice in her hometown. After sixteen years in private practice, she was offered the position of medical director at the community hospital in her hometown, which she accepted with enthusiasm.

She married a man three years her junior while she was in medical school. He was attending law school at the time, and he is now a moderately successful real estate attorney. Her children, two boys, were born about a year apart and are both accomplished percussionists in the high school band.

Personality: She is resourceful in solving new and challenging problems, preferring to move on to one new interest after another. She is quick and ingenious in finding logical solutions.

"We have a dedicated and committed medical staff, although they sometimes get distracted and lose their focus. I guess my concern over that challenge is the main reason that I was pleased to be invited to come to this conference. My primary responsibility is to the medical staff; however, when the hospital staff, especially the nurses, becomes unsettled, it affects the work of the medical staff directly. That is not to say that the doctors are not responsible for causing some of the unsettledness. Burnout, in particular, is an increasing distraction among doctors, and this also impacts the other members of the hospital staff. In fact, it almost always works in both directions, so I monitor the functioning of the entire operation. Anyway, we will be facing some major challenges in the near future. I have not had any formal education in management, but I have pretty good people skills. I had hoped that this conference would give me some insight into how I might best anticipate and be of assistance in the upcoming challenges facing the healthcare industry." She finished with a determined expression, apparently ready to meet those challenges here and now, if needed.

"Liz, what exactly are those challenges?" asked Dr. Bankston.

"They are primarily the new government regulations, and the mandate for Electronic Medical Record (EMR) implementation. The hospital is about 75 percent EMR compliant already, but in getting to that point we have encountered several challenges, so none of us look forward to going to 100 percent compliance. The big problem at the moment is in our medical practices. As is the trend nationally, we have purchased several physicians' offices in order to take over the management and insurance aspects—most of us MDs have undeveloped management skills—and getting them into compliance with these new laws is my responsibility. It will be a major undertaking and my biggest challenge yet. HELP!" Liz took her seat, smiling ruefully.

Joan, the first arrival at breakfast, spoke next. She had changed out of the gray suit and ruffled blouse, and was now in jeans and a sweatshirt. "I'll go next, if you all agree … is that okay? Well, my name is Joan, and I am the project manager for small-business development projects at a nationally recognized technology firm in North Carolina." At thirty-six, she was quite attractive, appearing physically fit and confidently assertive. "We specialize in the development and implementation of multi-dimensional organizational software systems. As an aside, Liz, even though we don't have any experience with medical systems, there are a few guidelines that I can share with you later that may help.

JOAN

Joan, thirty-six, grew up in relative affluence in an eastern North Carolina tobacco town. She attended private school and a women's college in Raleigh, where she majored in math with minors in accounting and Spanish. In rebellion to her upbringing, she joined the Peace Corps after graduation, served in rural Guatemala for two years, and then served stateside coordinating Peace Corps volunteer rotations to Spanish-speaking countries for two more years. She has a natural affinity for computer technology and spent much of her time installing and establishing a better system to track and communicate with volunteers in the field.

She returned to her hometown briefly to assist her father as he closed out the family tobacco processing company. Subsidies for tobacco crops were ending, and smaller operations had little or no future in the long term. She was able to organize the business in such a way that the operation was sold at a modest profit.

Two years ago, she was hired to manage software projects for small businesses and had managed to build this division of the company from an afterthought into one of its most profitable areas. Although she was not yet aware, she was presently being considered for a promotion to the position of a retiring vice president.

Personality: She is practical, realistic, and matter of fact, with a natural inclination for business solutions that are direct and have quick application. She is good at attending to details and moves quickly to make decisions.

"Anyway, the software systems that we deal with vary widely in required technological proficiency and according to organizational needs and complexity. This leads to one of our major challenges with our software trainers. We employ IT people to teach the new software programs to the client employees. Although changing to a new software program is not a problem for these employees, the trainer may not understand and become impatient with the client, if not outright intolerant. As a result, we may have relationship problems with some of our clients.

"In some ways I think I understand. Because I was a math major, my mathematical inclinations and my logical approach to problems always get in the way when trying to form a serious relationship. So, I am presently single, but I am still trying, so … HELP me, too!"

"Finally, a little humor—and from the mathematician at that—maybe there is some hope for this group after all," said

Dr. Bankston. Distant thunder rumbled in the background. "No, really, it's good that you are beginning to loosen up. We may need to take our goal and this weather seriously, but we should not take ourselves too seriously. Who's next?"

The young man from England introduced himself. "Hello, my name is Edward, and I am from Manchester, England. I am a systems engineer for a multinational corporation headquartered in the UK. Although working in Manchester at the moment, I am scheduled to be reassigned to our company's recently acquired US headquarters in the near future. It is in my nature to be flexible, but I admit that this situation is stretching me beyond my comfort zone.

EDWARD

Edward, thirty-two, is a systems engineer who was educated in the public school system in England and received his bachelor's and master's degree from a local university. He has been married seven years and has two small children, ages one and three. His wife has a dependent personality and still leans quite heavily on her parents for help with the children.

Edward began working as an intern with his present company while pursuing his graduate studies and has remained with that organization. After completing his education, he began working in quality control and was quickly thereafter promoted to project manager for review and recommendations regarding the present inventory system. This project was completed ahead of schedule and under budget. The projects he has been assigned since that time have been increasingly more critical to the success of the company, and most have been completed ahead of schedule and within or under budgetary projections.

He is unaware that he is presently on the short list of candidates for the new position of vice president of US operations. He would be the strongest candidate for the position, except for his age.

Personality: He is usually quiet and reserved, but has unexpected flashes of insight. Interested in cause and effect, he is good at getting to the core of a problem and finding the solution.

Underneath that wiry and tousled appearance was a compliant and unassuming personality. *No wonder he surprised himself with his declaration in the lobby on Friday night,* Dr. Bankston chuckled to himself, as Edward continued.

"My company's challenge is that they are always looking at the bottom line, and what will ostensibly save them a dollar here or a dollar there. I think your philosopher, Ben Franklin, had a saying about not being 'penny wise, but pound foolish,' and that seems to apply. So I am to go over to the US headquarters and immediately begin to implement our policies into their organizational structure. My first task is to implement a change in the way travel expenses are reported and reimbursed. This is just one prominent example that has immediately evident consequences.

"Their plans just do not make 'systems' sense, and they will cost them much more in the long run. What I mean is that an international acquisition is a new venture for my organization. We needed to expand, and this smaller US company was very successful in our field. I think we need to get to know this new division first and see why they are so successful. Perhaps there are things that they are doing that would help us be more competitive ourselves. Sure, they have made some mistakes, but while we are older and more established in the field, we are not mistake free ourselves. If I could just go over there and watch them for awhile to see how they have managed to succeed so quickly, I could blend a few of their procedures and protocols with ours, and perhaps we would all be better off as a result. I wish I could have just five minutes with the decision makers; I think I could cast a whole new light on these plans."

"Thank you, Edward, I will be anxious to hear more about your situation," replied Dr. Bankston. "But for now, let's hear from Hilde … have we saved the best for last?"

"Perhaps not, but I will say that having heard the others speak has given me a moment to pause and reflect," Hilde said, as a crimson blush appeared on her neck. She was a bit older than others in the group, and her demeanor seemed reserved. "I find it a bit hard to be as forthcoming as the rest of you. Although I am from Germany, if I am reserved it is not because of a language problem. My dad was transferred to New York when I was twelve, and I went to school here for four years before he was transferred back to Europe, so English is very natural for me. I'm the kind of person who would rather sit back in the shadows and not call attention to myself, but I can see that I will have to extend myself a bit in order to keep up with this group.

HILDE

Hilde was the youngest of three children from a middle-class German family. From the age of sixteen, she worked in her spare time with her father in his leather-working business. Although she was not allowed on the shop floor, she soon mastered the skill of producing many of the products by hand. Ultimately, however, it was the flow of the raw materials into the facility, the steps of manufacture, and the completion of the finished product that most fascinated her. By the time she had completed university with a degree in operations management, she had made suggestions that significantly improved the efficiency in her father's production assembly.

After her father's death, his business was closed, and she took a job working for one of her father's executives at a new facility, and where she still works for him. Because of his long friendship with her father, and also with her, she already dreads his impending retirement.

She has never married, and she had only once been in a serious relationship with a young man, but after his death in a tragic autobahn accident, she immersed herself in her work and never gave any evidence that she was seriously tempted by another relationship.

Personality: She succeeds by perseverance; she is quietly forceful, conscientious, and concerned about others. She is respected for her firm principles and clear vision regarding how to serve the common good.

"I am presently serving as an executive officer to the VP of production for a large manufacturing facility in Germany. Although we have been challenged lately, the organization has otherwise been consistently profitable during the ups and downs of the past fifteen years in large part because of the leadership of my boss. There are 1,683 employees in the production division with an average length of employment of over eight years—a remarkable achievement for this industry, but not so remarkable for my country. That is the positive aspect. Although it has not been announced yet, the downside is that my boss, the VP, is retiring at the end of this year, and I feel sure that our division will suffer as a result."

After Hilde finished speaking, Dr. Bankston appeared lost in thought. As he slowly rose to his feet, he mumbled to himself, "That was a lot to take in." Then a bit louder, he said, "I don't know about you, but I need a break, and some coffee. Who wants to join me?"

A bit confused as to why their introductions were so taxing, they obligingly paraded across the lobby to the breakfast room. This time they sat inside, as the rain was now beating persistently against the window. "Joe, can I reserve that table in the back for while?" asked Dr. Bankston. "I need some elbow room for the six of us, and a place to push some papers around. We'll need a pot of coffee, a pitcher of tea, and a few cups and glasses."

Joe, the head server, looked around as if he needed to find a space for them. The room was quite empty and was likely to remain so. He smiled. "Sir, you just go run off anyone in your way—whatever you want is yours. I'm here to help in any way I can."

"Thank you, Joe. In that case, do you also think you could bring us a tray of sandwiches and chips in thirty to forty-five minutes? It'll be near lunchtime by then. Any special requests? Vegetarian, allergies, etc.? No? Great—Joe, whatever is available will be fine. Take your time; it's still early and we are clearly in no big hurry."

DR. BANKSTON

Dr. Bankston was born during the middle of the Great Depression and raised in a rural town on the Texas-Oklahoma border. He was the only son of parents who worked hard to provide him the opportunity to escape the entrapments of the "dust bowl" and the dangers of the oil fields.

His inquiring and active mind did not lend itself to the level of devotion necessary to excel in the mundane and unchallenging aspects of the education process. However, even without any obvious effort in this regard, he still managed to gain admission to a major university. Here his curiosity was better challenged, and with increasing effort and dedication he worked his way up through a PhD in a field focused on group behavior and its relationship to management problems. The only thing that proved any distraction to this process was his marriage to his long-time sweetheart during the early years of his doctorate training.

After receiving his PhD, he accepted a temporary position in London, England at a human behavioral research institute. A few years later, he accepted a position at a major university back in the United States, where he has remained since that time. In addition to his teaching responsibilities, he consults on a regular basis to national and international clients and is the author of many papers and several books. Although approaching retirement age, he continues to maintain a vigorous schedule, as he attempts to find answers to problems that have plagued him throughout his career. And the problem at hand is the increasing turmoil in business and corporate cultures that has incrementally but perceptibly increased over the past thirty to forty years.

Personality: He is warmly enthusiastic, high spirited, ingenious, and imaginative. He is able to do almost anything that interests him, but it must first capture his attention. He often relies on his ability to improvise instead of preparing in advance. He finds solutions for most problems quickly and is ready to assist others when difficulties are encountered.

After about forty minutes or so of the conversations and cross-conversations that are all part of a small group getting to know one another, Joe reappeared with a cart loaded with trays of assorted sandwich-making materials and several types of pastries. "Help yourselves."

"Come on, join us, Joe. There is enough here for a small army. Here, take this table next to us."

Noon

As they all settled in to sandwich making, Dr. Bankston's mind wandered. *This sounds just like what I have been hearing from other participants all week. Everyone's challenges seem related to some kind of organizational change. But this relentless pace of change isn't going to let up anytime soon; it is necessary if an organization is going to remain competitive in the global marketplace? Maybe it is because the process for implementing a change project takes too long. Why is there such a struggle with change—why do employees seem to resist it so consistently everywhere?*

He then interrupted the idle chatter, "I can't quit thinking about what I have heard today. You have piqued my curiosity—I need to know more about your experiences. Please, talk to me for a little while longer about things at work." No one was immediately forthcoming. Lunch and the increasing intensity of the blowing rain seemed to be consuming all of their attention.

Although they were all still a bit confused, and more than a bit intimidated—at this moment more by Dr. Bankston than by the growing storm—Joan ventured forth first. "Well, I'm not sure how hearing more about my work problems will help anyone else. At least, it seems to me that all of our problems are different, and our organizations don't have very much in common. But here goes.

"Take our technical trainers, for example. They have always had a bit of a problem with our clients, especially during the software training and education phases. Of course, some of the trainers are more patient than others, but I mentioned that as a problem already. Although the trainers can get uptight, especially when an organization is not proficient in the use of computer-related technology, we are quite successful in our field. I do worry sometimes about their occasional snide remarks. I'm afraid that kind of elitist attitude may come back to haunt us someday.

"I guess my main concern lately has more to do with what is happening inside our company, rather than outside. There has been recently a general breakdown in our ability to function cohesively. For the most part we have a lot in common, and usually get along quite well; however, it has been pretty bad for the past month … everybody is on edge, and some have just withdrawn and retreated into their own private world …"

It's like it was this morning when we were outside. With the thunder in the distance, and the clouds rolling in … there was tension building in the air.

"Boy, that reminds me—here's a fiasco. Someone put the CFO at our company in charge of saving all of our work on the "Cloud". Now, there is concern about security, access, unauthorized document changes, etc.—everything is up in the air, pun intended, and no one knows what to do with what. The plan was to facilitate storage and access to information. But … well, to heck with it, someone else talk—now I am too irritated …"

Hilde raised her hand.

"Hilde, just jump in any time you feel like it," said Dr. Bankston, amused. "We're not that formal here. Go ahead."

"I'm not really shy, but I would normally just like to listen," explained Hilde. She paused. "I do not want to be confrontational myself, but something that Joan said sounded very familiar to me. Joan, we recently replaced our outdated software with a newer, more comprehensive technology. We have had some problems with profitability, and this was supposed to be an opportunity to streamline our operation. Unfortunately we also had to cut costs, and since we have a good internal change team, we decided to do most of the transition in house. We had good guidance about the mechanics of the process, but we had to cut back on the number of trainers and the time the trainers were onsite with our organization. I guess these trainers were technically competent, but they were rushed, and their impatient attitudes left us in a horrible state. That was four months ago now, and we are still having trouble using the software. To make matters worse, as I mentioned earlier, our production

VP has confided in me that he will be retiring at the end of this year, and he is the only thing that has been holding us together for the past few months. I am really stressed about my company, and maybe this is selfish, but in this EU economy, it is not the time to be out of a job ...."

"That's exactly what I'm facing if I move to the US," interjected Edward. "And all of this over saving a few dollars in travel costs. Here's just one little aspect of how irrational our new organizational process is. I don't know how I am going to sell this, but starting with the new fiscal year, no more travel can be charged to the company. At least forty percent of the management in this new US division travel on company business at least occasionally during the year. According to the new policy, soon to be in effect, when a trip is necessary, the employee will have to charge the travel, lodging, meals, and other expenses to his own credit card, and then submit receipts to the company for reimbursement.

"Now this works in England, not only has it been company policy for decades, but because travel costs are less in our country. Much of our travel is done by rail, so travel is easier and more efficient. Plus they travel more frequently over here, which may be part of this division's success, but distances in the US are much greater, so travel costs are that much higher. The central travel reimbursement office for now will still be headquartered in Manchester, and with the projected four-to-six-week delay in getting paid back for those expenses, it will introduce some significant hardships on those who travel regularly. The problems for me are huge, but potential problems for the company are worse. Since the announcement of these plans, even though most are acting as if nothing is going to happen, some are concerned, and others have even started looking for another job or are considering early retirement. I am afraid that the core of the division is either on the way out, or soon will be. That will be like taking the heart of the profit potential for this division and throwing it out the window ..."

Dr. Bankston turned to Jake. "Jake, you are looking confident. What do you have to say?"

"Well, I am thinking that having a job with the government have some advantages." Jake smiled self-consciously. "It is reasonably secure, even if the performance in my division has fallen off lately.

"But that does bring up a situation that I face, and we are also having a strong backlash. I mentioned earlier that I am challenged with the responsibility of explaining how the government application process, for certain services, works to the benefit of those in the public sector. Because of budget constraints, and without effective input from my department, a new system was designed and has now been implemented. This system has effectively removed the phone bank system and replaced it with a consumer information website that actually provides little or no information of value. Internally, employees have been reassigned and are angry about it, and that has created a real mess. If that's not enough, our complaint division has seen a massive escalation in the number of calls. The operators have not been trained to handle these calls, so that is creating a backlog of problems, and the morale in the office is plummeting.

"It may be good to have some level of job security, but I used to enjoy my work, and I even had a group from the other division that I liked to be around, but now they are having problems too. I go to lunch alone, my blood pressure is up, and I just dread Monday mornings. TGIF is my new mantra …"

"We are dealing with the same kinds of things in my world, too," Liz jumped in. "For example, we have a couple of newly acquired physician's offices that are rocky roads when it comes to change. It is interesting that the offices are so similar; however, their response to the new software system is so different—still resistant, but different.

"Let me give you an example. Our urology practice implemented its new software a couple months ago. One of their doctors decided to retire about that time to make room for the two new doctors who were hired to assist the remaining urologist with the heavy work load. We felt that with the transition, this would be a good time to introduce the new software. They seem to have adapted well to software changes, but this previously friendly office has suddenly become impatient and abrupt with their patients. That is just not like them at all.

"By contrast, in our newly acquired neurology clinic, we introduced the same software just about the same time, with the same trainers and the same training period. For some reason they are far behind the urology practice in getting the software up and running. It is interesting that the practices are about the same size, three doctors each, and about the same number of employees. Here morale is fine, but productivity has fallen—by that I mean they are seeing fewer patients per day—otherwise things seem to be going smoothly.

"The hospital is plugging along pretty good, but with these two experiences, I am anxious about what to expect when we tackle the compliance issues at the hospital in a few months."

Dr. Bankston leaned back in his chair and thought a moment. "Well, when I asked the five of you to give me some stuff to think about, you sure did it. There is something bouncing around in my head, but I can't yet seem to put my finger on it. On the surface, each scenario is totally unique, but under the surface, the dynamics seem so similar. Strange. I wonder if all of this unsettled behavior is just the result of change … but the change is in many forms. Change in leadership, change in technology, change in protocol or process, change in location …"

He thought to himself, *If this is a struggle with change, it is not just consistent—it's universal and intense. But why?*

He seemed to abruptly come to a decision. "How about a bit of homework? Anyone interested? I am writing some references down. Each of you take an article or two, do some Internet searches on them, and let's get back together tonight— here at the corner offices of Bankston and Company at 5:30. No, considering the storm, we had better meet in the small interior room across the lobby, next to the room where we met this morning. I have a good feeling about this—no, not the hurricane, but the conversation. Who knows? We might be on the verge of a discovery."

After each person had copied their references and went off to do their research, Dr. Bankston called out across the dining room: "Joe, do you have a replacement coming in this afternoon?"

"I was supposed to be replaced at three o'clock, but I called him and told him I would stay through the night. Several of the other kitchen staff and one or two from hotel guest services will stay, too. No reason to go home when we have a big, empty, safe hotel to stay in. Not too many times that I get to stay in a hotel—I might even use one of the guest rooms. My supervisor said it would be okay. I guess you know that there are a few other guests at the hotel that also need to be taken care of. It looks like I will be on duty tomorrow, too."

"What do you have in mind for dinner?"

"Sir, Benjamin here and I have been talking. He was a Navy cook for six years. Served on a submarine, and you might not know it, but those are some of this country's best cooks. He doesn't often get to do much cooking on his own around here, but if you are flexible, I think we can make it worth the effort. What do you say about that?"

"With a Navy cook, and enough food for half the Navy, I sure it will be fantastic. Joe, you said that seven employees will be staying at the hotel tonight, and eight to ten guests? Okay, I'll call the manager on call for the hotel this weekend. If any of you who are staying here tonight want to have your families join you, I'll work with the manager to make that happen. But get them here soon; this hurricane is supposed to get much worse before long. Whoever comes can join in the feast, and please invite those other guests that are stuck here; let them join us too. The food is all paid for anyway, and as long as you want to do the work, it's okay with me."

The Evening—5:30 p.m.

As the delicious smells of the upcoming feast drifted into the lobby, the group found themselves wandering into the appointed meeting room earlier than scheduled. Everyone was present when Dr. Bankston arrived at precisely 5:30 p.m. "I trust you all had an interesting and productive afternoon, and maybe even a little time for a rest. Let's not get into your afternoon research until after dinner. Joe and Benjamin have really created an incredible feast with scrumptious surprises for us. Rumor has it this has become a family affair, so dig in and enjoy."

The meal was more than was promised. In addition to Benjamin and Joe, two of the wives and one of the guests also joined in the cooking—and it was fantastic. In fact, there was so much food, the nearby fire department and a couple police patrol cars were asked to join in the festivities. The food and fun, however, could not drown out the persistent roar of the wind.

At 7:15 p.m., Dr. Bankston interceded. "The hurricane is supposed to peak in a couple hours, and considering our level of distraction with that, and our now-full stomachs, I'm afraid that if we don't get started soon, we never will. What say we adjourn to the conference room for a short session, and that we keep the discussion to the basics this evening? For those who are interested, the hurricane-watch party can reconvene at about 9:00 p.m. Come on, now— and for goodness' sake, don't forget your little hurricane charms."

"Yipes, I left mine up in the room," grimaced Liz.

Joan leaned over and whispered, "Better go get it—I'll let the others know you're coming."

As Liz bolted for the elevator, the rest of the group followed Dr. Bankston across the hall to the boardroom. Dr. Bankston turned around. "Is Liz alright?"

"Yes—she just went to get her hurricane charm. Does she need it?" asked Joan.

Dr. Bankston nodded seriously. "She may, indeed." The group exchanged glances, and then each subtly checked to be sure they had their packages as well. Inside the conference room, they found their seats around the table. Liz suddenly appeared, breathless, at the door, and held up her box triumphantly. Several clapped as Liz found her place at the table.

"Very good," said Dr. Bankston. "Who wants to start? Edward?"

"Yes, I had some Kurt Lewin references," said Edward, narrowing his gaze on his laptop screen as he brought up his notes. "He is generally considered to be the father of change management. He introduced a linear pattern to the change process, which proved to be of considerable benefit, initially. His work, though, has now been superseded by some more recent stuff. In a nutshell, he said that change is a three-stage process. The first stage is 'unfreezing.' It starts by overcoming the 'status quo.' In the second stage, the change occurs. This is a period of transition where the old patterns are beginning to be replaced by new patterns, and a great deal of confusion may exist in the individual. The third stage he called 'freezing,' during which the individual once again begins to achieve a comfort level (*Wikipedia*, s.v. "Kurt Lewin"). I might not know much about change, but from what I have seen, this guy sure got the part right about the confusion."

"Well, perhaps we see a pattern developing," said Dr. Bankston. The other group members agreed—they were engaged now. "Liz, you had the first Bowlby reference. Why don't you go next?"

"John Bowlby, an Englishman, worked for decades on something he called 'attachment theory.' He said that we all have in our basic nature at birth an obsession to become attached to things. These tendencies to attach are healthy in the best of circumstances. The interesting part for me was that he found that these tendencies were present throughout childhood, adolescence, and even in adults. If I understood correctly—some of it was over my head— the mourning process is just one easily identifiable example of adult attachment behavior. That sounded at least a little like the confusion described by Lewin."

At this point, Hilde jumped into the discussion. "I agree, Liz; it is like some type of confusion and a lot like mourning, too—and it really goes together with what I found. In my article, Bowlby (1980, 9–41) emphasized that it is a distinct form of behavior that is natural for our species and involves very intense emotions. He later also goes on to recognize and significantly expand the definition of attachment behavior, especially in adults, to include groups and organizations— in addition to the family, to objects such as a familiar place or social role (245–246), and to inanimate objects when the 'natural' object is unavailable" (1969, 312). Hilde stopped suddenly, aware that she had interrupted Liz, and apologized.

Dr. Bankston laughed. "Good for you, Hilde; I think this group stuff is good for you. Now Joan, did you have the Harvey readings?"

"Yes, I found some interesting information in a synopsis of Jerry Harvey's book, *How Come Every Time I Get Stabbed in the Back, My Fingerprints Are on the Knife?* Have any of you ever read any of his stuff? He is a bit near the fringes for me—you should read what he says about "not*teaching." I never had a teacher like that.

"But to get back to the point, in this book Dr. Harvey has revived a concept called 'anaclitic depression.' This term was originally used by Rene Spitz in reference to his research in orphanages in the 1940s. It describes a depression that results when access to something or someone that was previously 'leaned on' is lost. Harvey (1999) has now adopted the term to describe a particular form of 'the blues' that occurs when individuals, organizations, or belief systems that we lean on or are dependent on for emotional support are withdrawn from us. For instance, when we are put down by someone in a leadership role, or go through the trials and tribulations of an organizational downsizing, or suffer through a corporate reorganization over which we have no control, or have to relinquish a cherished belief system, we often suffer from what he called the ravages of the 'anaclitic depression blues.'

"That's it, that's all from me. But really, I do have to say that while this is all very interesting, I am not sure I can see the point. I will say that the Harvey readings sound a lot like the attachment article Liz and Hilde talked about, but how is it related to the mysterious causes of your pervasive, unhealthy organizational environment? To me, it just seems like this is distracting us from the real issue. My question is, how do we go about solving the problem?"

"Joan, let me wait a minute before I respond to you. I see that Jake is eager to get started?"

"Well, I had the references on change models, and I don't know about this attachment and depression stuff, and I think Lewin may have had the right idea, but it is out of date," said Jake, scanning his notes.

"But some of the newer change methodologies seem to be bringing Lewin's stuff more up to date. They say implementing a change initiative is a multi-step process that makes people want to change. If people see the need for change, if their bosses support it, talk it up, and make a mental image of the good that will result from the change, that will start the ball rolling. Then you remove the obstacles that develop, and produce evidence of the positive results that are occurring to help build a positive image. In turn, the new image then becomes a part of the culture of the organization that can help the employees develop a new sense of pride. I'll admit it seemed easier when I was reading about it than when I just described it, but it does really make sense. What do you all think?"

Dr. Bankston responded. "Jake, I agree, and for the benefit of all of you, the ideas contained in these general change models are not the only good ones. There are similar change protocols from John Kotter, Prosci and Jeff Hiatt, Daryl Conner, William Bridges, Jim Collins, and many, many others, and they all make good sense and are important considerations that have been developed over the past fifteen to twenty years or so.

"But there is one little problem. Even when people try to follow the these very sensible methodologies, researchers have shown that there is still a failure rate well above 50% for most new organizational change initiatives (Standish 2015; Standish 2009; IBM 2008; Raps 2004; Beer 2003; HBR 1998; Senge 1999; Strebel 1996; and Kotter 1995). There is some mystery component missing from their formulas, and I can think of nothing I would rather do on this stormy weekend, when we have been abandoned by so many of our esteemed colleagues, than to find at least one of those missing pieces of the puzzle. And I think the articles you've reviewed today may prove to be the key.

"Joan, to answer your question about how these ideas practically relate to the solution, I'm beginning to think that your Cloud scenario and Liz and Hilde's software changes may be less about the Cloud and the new software. What if the critical part is not so much getting prepared for and adjusting to something new, like the methodologies that Jake reviewed, but is more importantly about what they are losing? This really could be more about the old stuff being 'lost' or left behind as a result of the change. We may actually have been looking for the real issues in the wrong place, and maybe the real issues are not the ones we always thought they were. It's really something new to think about.

"With that being said, I have a personal story to share with you." Dr. Bankston cleared his throat. "I have been unsettled myself for several months now. My basement office has always been a sort of sanctuary for me, but lately I have not been comfortable there. I could not figure out what the problem was—that is, until today, when I saw Joan get mad at the cloud. That started me thinking, and it led to my recollection of those articles that I asked each of you to look into.

"So, here's a confession. Recently I retired my home computer—old 'Betsy.' She was so much a part of the accomplishments of my life that, I am humbled to admit, I was unable to let go, at least unconsciously.

"But I think I can now. What if, to paraphrase Pogo, 'the enemy is me' or at least within me? This afternoon while you were working on those references, I called Barbara, my wife, and asked her to take my old computer out of the box to be thrown away and instead put 'her' up on the shelf. Not on my desk, but on the shelf, with my family photos and other memorabilia.

"I must tell you that I feel better already. My old computer may be retired, but I'm not going to throw her away. And I am not ready to throw in the towel, and I am not going to fully retire—at least not yet. I have a few more things yet to accomplish, and this weekend has now become the celebration of whatever I have left to finish. Thank you all for being a part of it and for being an incentive that helped make it happen.

"Now, on to your question: yes, I think these articles are not distractions from the real issue of making change initiatives work, but may provide the very insights that could explain the mystery of just why so many change initiatives fail.

"But not tonight. It is getting late for an old man like me. The storm is intensifying, and I also have a few phone calls to make. I think the hotel staff is going to have an impromptu hurricane watch that you are welcome to join if you so desire. Enjoy yourselves, but be careful. Don't stay up too late because we will reconvene at 7:30 a.m., weather permitting. By then, each of you should be ready to describe in newfound language what is going on in your organization. See you in the breakfast room. Be ready and be sharp! We'll have a lot of ground to cover in a short period of time."

Sunday Morning—7:30 a.m.

When everyone awoke the next morning, they could immediately tell that the wind was much subdued. After getting a cup of coffee from the lobby, Dr. Bankston walked into the meeting room, right on time as usual, and surveyed the group.

"It seems morning came early today, and judging from the baggy eyes staring at me, sleep must have been scarce. Seems the storm was not as bad as feared, but it did get my attention from time to time. They say the worst is over. Joe, how did the storm watch go last night? Any harrowing adventures to speak of?"

Joe spoke up. "Well, we did have some excitement at about two o'clock this morning. We were all getting tired of the storm watch, and since there were only twelve of us, including our families, we pulled some furniture into a group in the lobby and planned to sleep there. Anyway, we were all trying to calm down my little girl, Marie. She's four, but she wouldn't settle down without her 'Patty.' That's her little cloth doll that she's slept with since she was a baby, and she forgot to bring it. She was really upset about it. I'm sure she was insecure about the storm too, but last night that doll was all she wanted—she was inconsolable.

"It was while that was going on that a lightning bolt hit the tree around on the other side—shook the hotel so bad I thought it was an earthquake. Well, it was quite a scene—the tree was split wide open and pieces of bark lying all around, some pieces smoking. We all stood around and watched long enough to satisfy our curiosity, then went back to our nesting area, and Marie was gone.

"Well, it was panic time … it took us almost an hour to find her. We knew she couldn't have gone outside since the doors are locked, so we weren't completely panicked"—Hilde and Joan exchanged knowing smiles—"but we were getting pretty anxious, and we were about to call our friends from the fire department, when someone noticed that the gift shop door had been left open. We looked inside, and there on the floor, lying on top of a big Raggedy Ann doll, was my little Marie, sound asleep.

"I can already tell Raggedy Ann won't ever replace Patty, but it got her through the night. I guess all's well that ends well, but we sure didn't get much sleep. I do want to especially thank Joan and Hilde. They stayed up much of the night talking, and were actually the ones who first spotted Marie in the gift shop."

Hilde smiled. "We started talking and let time slip up on us, and we were more than glad to help when Marie turned up missing. But you're welcome, Joe. We did a good night's work, didn't we, Joan?"

Joan laughed and nodded in agreement. "I suppose we did, and in more ways than one."

Joe continued, "If I am a little slow this morning, I apologize, but if I can get together some coffee and sodas and a few of the leftover pastries, will that be enough for an hour or two? We'll put together a big brunch for you if you can wait until, say, about ten-thirty to eat. Meanwhile, while they are working in the kitchen, if it's okay with you, I'll just sit over here so I can get you anything else you may need."

They all nodded their heads in agreement, as Dr. Bankston reassured Joe that those plans were perfectly satisfactory. Then he turned back to the group. "All's well that ends well, indeed. I hear they will try to open the airport later this afternoon, so if we are going to wrap up this mystery, we'd better get started.

"I think Jake was one of the last ones to speak last night; should we go backwards in our order of speaking this morning? Jake, are you ready?"

Jake was still thinking about Joe's story. "Wow, I had no idea that all happened last night—I slept through everything. Even a hurricane is quieter than my neighbors at home, I can tell you. But I did see the tree this morning; there's a mess out in the courtyard.

"But yes, I am ready to talk about my agency's problem. Based on what we have found out so far, I suspect my department just had too much change at one time—the new website, the removal of the phone bank, no training for dealing with the issues that would have been previously handled by the phone bank operators, escalation of the calls to the complaint division…That was a lot to take on, especially without any input into the changes. It might have taken us a while, but we could have insured that the information on the website at least addressed the issues that were previously handled by the phone bank. It was not handled at all well. What do you think, Dr. Bankston?"

"Hmmm … I'll wager you stayed up awhile last night and did some work on this project, didn't you? Well, Jake, I think you are pretty close. Of course, we have no way of identifying the problem precisely, but I'd say there was probably too much change and too little preparation—but let me get back to that later. I want to hear what all of you have to say first. Joan, you were next, weren't you?"

"Well, if we are going in reverse order, I guess I am," Joan said. "Dr. Bankston, the five of us stayed in here and talked for an hour or so after you left last night, before we joined the rest of the watch party in the lobby. Here is my best guess, based on what we talked about last night.

"I think most, if not all, of the problems at my company are related to the decision to use cloud-based storage. Maybe it was a good idea to promote access to more information for those who are busy with a client. We even did fairly well at announcing the change and providing training. The problem was that the CFO who decided on using the Cloud apparently never took into account how this could be used and misused.

"We even did fairly well at announcing the change and providing training. I think we would have still had problems. The company has always had security concerns, and even many in IT keep private documents, such as passwords, on USB or password protected local information so they can work at home. It also likely means the IT people are now also responsible for teaching those employees with less technological knowledge in our company. So far the company has not adopted a consistent policy regarding data storage, so there are many loop holes that can be exploited. Maybe I am just too independent, but having this choice made on my behalf truly unsettled me."

"Good, Joan, but you really had an easy one to figure out. Hilde, I think you are up next."

"Dr. Bankston, I think I have double trouble. I see now that the software introduction has taken a lot of the energy from those in my division—I think they have a case of the 'blues,' like we said earlier, and if the VP retires as planned, I think we are in for some even worse times ahead. Dr. Bankston, we are already on the edge financially; do you have any suggestions about how to limit some of the effects of these symptoms? We really need to be able to improve productivity."

"Hilde, I have a few ideas, but I would rather wait until the others finish, and then I may add a thought or two. Liz, you ready?"

"Well, where do I start, and with which set of problems? I have Urology; I have Neurology. I have the nursing staff at the hospital, and then I have the medical staff at the hospital, and that is just for starters. If there is something to this depression or attachment concept, then that will be a starting point.

Whatever I do, I will promise to send you all an update later, whether it works out or not. Meantime, I am interested to see what Edward has to say."

"That's all right, Liz. You've got the floor, Edward," interjected Dr. Bankston.

"It looks like I have some leadership problems and some communications problems with my superiors," said Edward. "Someone must be feeding them some erroneous information, and as process implementation manager for the new US division and for this new travel policy, I think I need to get on the agenda of the next VPs' meeting. This may be a change that never needs to happen. Some damage has already been done, but it may be reversible. We will have plenty of opportunities to evaluate the impact of change on my company if we just take our time and try to learn as much as we can about the new division and about ourselves before we take an irreversible course."

"Edward, I wondered how you would approach your problem. I agree this is a leadership issue, and since there is still time, the cards are all on your table. If you tell your boss about our "organizational storm" workgroup, maybe that will get you in front of the VPs' council. And I'll have a few more comments a little later."

Dr. Bankston—9:00 a.m.

"Well, it seems that each of you did a good job of summarizing your organizational scenarios. When I went back to my room last night, I decided to do a bit more digging on my own; it's taken me a bit more time to put all of this together than it has taken you. But the thing that has been on my mind is that there seems to be a common thread connecting all of you, and many of the others that attended this conference as well.

"In particular, I really sensed a connection between the problems we face and what Harvey was saying. So I called a young colleague who worked with Dr. Harvey. In her dissertation, she worked to extend the concept of anaclitic depression blues more specifically to organizational change, and in so doing she generated the Model of an Organizational Loss of Effectiveness (LOE). I wanted to see what connections, if any, she had found in her subsequent research. When I called her, I struck the jackpot, so to speak. In fact, she sent me an e-mail with a good summary of her information (for a copy of this e-mail, see Appendix C). I think I now have an explanation for many of the problems we have been concerned with at the conference and in our group. Perhaps I can explain on a preliminary level how these problems can be prevented, or at least minimized, in the future. Let's see if I understand it well enough to explain it to you.

"Before I go too far, let me say that if she is right, and I think she may very well be, the difficulty that we all are having with our organizations and change can be summed up in one word—*attachments*. It is in our nature as humans to develop an attachment to things that we lean on for support, and we do not want to lose touch with those things. We learned a little about this last night with the Bowlby and Harvey reports, but it goes so much further than that.

"It is easy to understand the attachment between a mother and her child, or between spouses, or even with pets, for goodness' sake. And when we lose one of these attachment 'objects,' we go through a period of mourning—it is expected, it is normal, and it is healthy. It now seems apparent that in an organization, we also form attachments, or become dependent on things. It may be obvious when we become attached to a boss, a colleague, or even a work group.

"The problem is that we do not just form attachments to pets or individuals or groups of people. We can form attachments to objects, tangible and intangible, that have become important to us and may even help us do our jobs. We can form attachments to a particular office space, a computer (like I did with my Betsy), and even the software that we use to do our reports. We can also become attached to abstract concepts or experiences, such as a view out of a certain window, or to rules, protocols, and policies. Anything that we identify with as providing security, familiarity, and/or stability in our work lives can be an object of attachment, and that really complicates things.

"To understand why we form these attachments, we have to look far back into our history to the groups that still live in the shadows of our modern world, and we will see that for most of human existence, change is first experienced as a 'loss.' In the earliest of times, we had few, if any, frivolous possessions. Whatever we possessed was of critical importance for our survival. In that case, a loss precipitated a change in the status quo, and as such was a threat to our survival. As a result, there has developed within us a warning system—a sense of insecurity or instability that resulted from the fact that change had become associated with a survival risk.

"That reaction is so deeply embedded in our nature that, even today, the threatened removal or replacement of something in our organizations that we've come to depend on triggers an urgent reaction designed to remove the threat or help us avoid it. The source of the problem is not so much the new object, but the threat of the loss of the old one. It is simply not in our nature to easily accept any change associated with loss; based on our developmental history, confronting change causes a natural but intense inner turmoil or sense of foreboding. During a major organizational change, this sense of turmoil is universal among employees, whether they understand the reasons behind the change or not, and symptoms of this turmoil eventually lead to behaviors that can undermine the purposes of the organization. This is called an 'organizational loss of effectiveness,' or 'organizational LOE'—and it really does feel 'low,' doesn't it?

"As far as what the symptoms look like, I think we've seen examples in each of your organizations' reactions to change. So you've already experienced how difficult this problem really is, but what's just now becoming clear is how simple it

"The difficulty with change can be summed up in one word... *attachments.*"

is to understand. The really good news is that there now is a way of measuring these symptoms, the behaviors that result, and preventive steps that can be taken to mitigate and/or prevent the problems they cause. The quantitative metric was originally named the LOE Index (LOE, of course, meaning 'loss of effectiveness'), however it was renamed the **CHANGE DIAGNOSTIC INDEX (CDI)** after a revision in 2015.

"It is simply amazing to me how it all fits together. Group, this is cutting-edge stuff. It has been published in several places, but it has been slow to filter into use in organizations. It isn't even being taught much in business schools yet. Perhaps that is about to change. Jake, you will be glad to know that it will not replace the existing methodologies that you reviewed; it should, however, become a critical component in those processes. It is exciting stuff that I am sure will lead to the correction of many woes associated with organizational change. It won't altogether stop the feelings of turmoil and restlessness that accompany a change event—after all, we can't change human nature—but understanding its influence will certainly help us deal with it better.

"The bottom line is that change is going to cause problems for the company, at least in the short run. How long the short run lasts, and how significant the impact of the change, will depend on a number of factors. And we now know that one important factor is understanding how change impacts the individual. Knowing this is basic to improving the success and minimizing the costs associated with any change initiative."

Hilde, with a sudden shake of her head, jumped in. "Dr. Bankston, that is more than I can take in at one time. Can you simplify or summarize what you just said, for those of us who are not native English speakers?"

"Okay, Hilde. I am excited about what I have learned, but I will try to cut it down to the bottom line, so we can get to some of your questions.

"What I think we have found out is that any change or threat of change that disturbs the status quo will cause instability in the organization. This is because change threatens to remove things that we've become attached to and that we lean on for support. The tendency to attach to things is inherent in the nature of *all* people—not just in infants and those with dependent personalities—and when an attachment is threatened, it results in an instability that spreads throughout the organization. This instability leads to the onset of symptoms, like lower morale, absenteeism, decreased motivation, decreased productivity, increased conflict, etc. The emergence of these symptoms then leads to behaviors that result in the organization being less effective than it might be otherwise. All of these factors lead to a generalized sense of unrest, in us and collectively through us in the organization.

"To go just a little further, it seems that our lives are all about attachments. We can't rationalize or wish away these attachments, because they are part of our internal defense mechanisms. So when we face change, the price we pay for the change is a period of unrest or instability. If we are to face this honestly, we must accept and deal with the pain of change as a natural part of the change process, and of life. If we deny this pain, or pretend change doesn't affect us, we find ourselves at the point described by Dr. Carl Jung, when he observed that a 'neurosis (instability) is always the substitute for legitimate suffering.'

"Let me tell you how my thoughts are evolving because of what we are now learning. I now am beginning to believe that this feeling of unrest in today's organization arises from the frequency of change that is necessary to remain competitive in today's world. I believe that this discontentedness is a side effect of our unwillingness as individuals and organizations to face and deal with the internal or subjective component of organizational change. As a consequence, we find what amounts to a neurosis pervading our businesses and industries. I believe that this has its origins in the same feelings of unrest that lead to the behaviors that cause a loss of effectiveness, and that eat away at the profits of the organization. But just as with a neurosis, if we are willing to accept and deal honestly with our human nature, many things can be done to prevent or at least limit the extent of the problems encountered."

Dr. Bankston's Summary—9:45 a.m.

"Looking at the time, and based on the smells from the kitchen, if you will allow me the privilege, I will try to summarize where we have come so far, and how your cases might relate to what we now suspect to be the case. Now of necessity, these evaluations will be simplistic and incomplete, but they should be enough to show you what is possible with the additional details provided by the concept of the organizational LOE and its correlation with attachment theory. Is that okay with everyone?

Dr. Bankston began writing on the conference whiteboard (Table 1)."First, let me show you how my colleague's email relates the six individual symptoms that occur due to loss of an "attachment" to their organizational equivalents."

"Does this shed some light on what we have been discussing so far? We can't really see or measure the individual symptoms of change, but I think we see their effects when we discuss the organizational challenges you are experiencing.

"So now let's try to apply this to what you are seeing in your organizations. Jake, let's start with you. If we take what we have discovered and apply it to your department, I think you are right: your department is the victim of change. The changes I heard you mention earlier this morning were first, the elimination of the phone bank that was apparently doing a pretty good job of handling questions; second, the creation of a website that was supposed to handle questions but is failing to do so; and finally, the reassignment of the displaced personnel. Is that correct?"

"Yes, sir—that, plus the calls to the complaint division, and the lack of training for the workers who were reassigned from the phone bank to other positions."

"Jake, I think your department had only one change, and no effective methodology. The elimination of the effective phone bank and its replacement with a new but ineffective website was the only change, but it has had a domino effect and spread into other areas of your department. Most of these problems come from the failure to use an effective protocol to prepare for and introduce the change.

"Based on what we are learning here, perhaps the protocol was never developed because no one accounted for the instability the change would inherently cause. An effective protocol would have allowed departmental input and thoughtfulness to enter the decision-making process. This could have led to a more gradual transition, training and re-education classes, a more useful website, and things such as that.

"So I really do think it was the lack of proper protocol for the elimination of the phone bank that was the major cause of all the problems. This, plus the change itself, has caused things to escalate out of control. It would have been really interesting if we had quantitative metric scores and could look back and see the state of mind in your division before the changes and follow it into the present. I suspect the intensity of the reaction is a sign that there was already instability in your department before the change ever happened.

"If I knew the specific symptoms I might be of more assistance, but I will hazard a guess that almost all of the attachment symptoms are now in an escalated position. It seems obvious that there are problems that have led to *lower morale.* I think this is due in large part to your division being left out of the loop on the important decisions. It would of course been better to involve them from the start, but their morale will improve somewhat if they can see you and your director getting involved on addressing an internal resolution of the present problems.

"*Absenteeism* relates not only to being physically absent from work, but also to daydreaming, planning a vacation, or anything that distracts someone's thought process from the work task at hand. This is often a problem when employees feel unimportant or left out, so get them involved with you as you address these problems.

"You said they sometimes act as if they have given up, and that they don't seem to have any empathy with applicants. This is probably related to problems relating to *motivation*—and involving them in individual and group coaching efforts should also lead to some improvements. You also said you had some anger issues. That is a sign of *conflict* and would respond to better communications, which, as you also noted, was a particularly apparent problem of late.

There may have also been some increased *loss of productivity*, but that was less apparent.

"Addressing these problems, all of which may relate back to the loss of the phone bank and the inadequacies in the website, would be time well spent. Even so, I think your Fridays will continue to come slowly for at least a few months. As best I could tell, those are the main issues, but as we discuss some of the others' problems, you will probably pick up some more pointers as well.

"Joan, I think you actually had one of the easier problems. So, I'll try to help you with your company's problem first, but I can't be quite so helpful with your love life—you're on your own there. I think your problems resulted from the company's change to storing information on the Cloud. It seems that the changes inherent in moving information to the Cloud has affected the atmosphere in your company, especially IT. Based on what I now know, I also expect the problems are as much about the additional work loads, the possible loss of access, some issues about control, new questions about personal and organizational security, and sorting out the conveniences and inconveniencies that will be confronted.

"Joan, I hope you will take back the message to your co-workers that change is hard for everyone. I think you should point out that changes in the way information is stored has led to the organizational equivalent of *conflict*, and is the cause of some contentiousness. This is a direct result of perceived losses associated with moving information storage to the Cloud. The lack of input from the users and the internal mandate of acceptance from your CFO have likely impacted or will soon impact organizational *morale*.

"Also, I expect that you have experienced some *decreased productivity*, similar to what we discussed with Jake. You didn't say anything to indicate that it was a problem, but I wouldn't be surprised. I think that you should work to make sure that this experience will have a positive effect on your trainers. Perhaps they will become more patient and tolerant if they see they are not immune to the problems of having to change technologies. Based on this experience, maybe they can now understand that when they introduce your software product to your clients, they are inadvertently causing the same experience.

"As far as the disruption in your company is concerned, let's just address the *conflict* for now. As I have said, there may be more issues involved, but based on this information, I would suspect that a staff meeting might be a great place to start. If given the opportunity, communicating with each other, and having management listen and learn from this experience, might allow a quicker return to a more normal and cooperative business environment."

"Thank you, Dr. Bankston, and I think you are right on all accounts: the solution of the company's problems may be easy compared with my personal one," Joan replied, smiling. "I appreciate your interest in us, and the opportunity that we have all shared, more than you will ever know. Thank you."

"You are surely welcome, Joan. Please let me know how it turns out for you.

"Hilde, if I remember, you have two changes to deal with: one just past and one on the horizon, and this situation does present a difficult problem. As far as the software introduction is concerned, I think you had a pretty good implementation protocol, except for the lack of trainers. That likely resulted in *decreased productivity* because the individual responses to

Figure 1

Anxiety leads to lower
Morale in the Organization.

Employee *Frustration* leads to
Organizational *loss of Productivity*.

Retardation of Development
(employees stop caring)
leads to decreased *Motivation*.

Rejection of the Environment
(if employees are mad about the change)
leads to increased *Conflict*.

Refusal to Participate means
increases in *Absenteeism*
(includes day dreaming at work).

Withdrawal means looking for
a way out or higher *Turnover*.

inadequate training were probably not adequately anticipated. The good news is that the change impact from this should be calming down in the near future. If you use some of your better operators to provide supplemental training to those operators who still seem to be having problems, then I expect productivity will increase accordingly. Obviously, qualitative interviews or the Change Diagnostic Index would have helped, but looking ahead, I hope that it may be possible for you to introduce it during the next change event. I will give you the e-mail address of the colleague I mentioned earlier so you can contact her and investigate what type of protocol for the Organizational LOE is available in your language.

"My most significant concern for you is the retirement of the VP and the potential impact on the *organizational morale*. Based on what I have guessed from hearing you speak, this will be a difficult adjustment for the production division to handle. This is especially so since they are in recent recovery from another difficult change. There is such a thing as recency bias, which means that one bad change experience will often cause employees to anticipate that another change experience will also be difficult. This expectation of difficulties might cause an escalation of problems beyond what might have otherwise been expected. This is more often true when the changes are similar in type, but in this case, I fear that your division may be unavoidably biased.

"My suggestion is that you talk to the VP and see if he could take a leave of absence for six months before he announces his retirement. That may give your employees time to adjust to someone new and make the transition less difficult. This proactive measure for slowly decreasing dependence on the VP will, hopefully, circumvent the potential for *morale* challenges to develop within the organization. This may be a bit presumptuous, but I suspect that you have a really good relationship with the various production crews. In that case, it might be natural to appoint you as an interim liaison for that position. Also, because I know you are concerned about the critically low productivity level, if you use your best operators to do some in-house training, that should help. And if you can swing it, I'll be glad to work with you when the time comes to see if we can find a way to anticipate and moderate the reaction."

"Thank you, Dr. Bankston, but I hope you are not giving me too much credit."

"Hilde, you are much more capable than you believe, and you seem to have the gift of insight. It sounds to me as if Joan and you have found some common ground for communication. It might do you both good to stay in touch with each other."

Dr. Bankston turned to Edward. "Edward, we have talked about most of your issues. I do not need to point out that the travel reimbursement decision, if carried out, could lead to a potential problem with distracted behavior that could manifest itself in the form of *absenteeism* and ultimately *increased turnover*. For this new division, the people who travel have relationships that will take a long time to replace. They will be attractive candidates for your competitors also, so they are likely to find jobs even in the current economic climate. You'll want to point this out at the upcoming executive committee meeting.

"I will have a few more comments later—because of the timing, your position, and the size of your organization, please pay close attention. You are in a very interesting position. If you can get your organization's executive committee to understand the information we have discussed over the last twenty-four hours related to attachment theory, I think you can strengthen the *morale* in the organization and ultimately introduce a solid foundation for current and future successful ventures."

"Yes sir, I understand," said Edward. "I know what I have to do; delay the change, and then see if I can adjust the strategy to integrate a travel reimbursement process that will support and meet the needs of both profitability and people. In the meantime, I need to learn all that I can about attachments and attachment behavior."

"That leaves you, Liz."

"Dr. Bankston, I think I have a solution to my problem staring me in the face," Liz said, laughing. "Do you think *you* might be available to consult with me and my hospital? My problems run too deep and I have too many aspects for me to handle without help."

"Well, you might know more than you think you know. First, let's talk about what you have related to us here: your two medical offices. They are interesting contrasts in response to the technology change, and we should be aware of those differences. Consider the urology group. They added two new doctors, and the older doctor retired at the same time. Even with one doctor remaining, this was a dramatic leadership change. On top of that, somebody made the 'interesting' decision to add a software technology change at the same time. It is no wonder that they have *morale* issues because of the change in leadership. I suspect that they had rather significant issues with *absenteeism* that, if left unresolved, could lead to the *turnover* of several very important clinicians and office management staff. When you get back, check and see if they have any *conflict* issues— I'll wager they would benefit from a series of office meetings to improve communications between the staff and the new doctors, and probably a big office party to welcome and get to know the new doctors and honor the one who retired. It is a testament to a strong and positive culture in that clinic that they held together at all.

"Now, the neurology clinic is a lesson in how things can work better. But based on what you said, I would bet that this office did not have the same confidence with computers that the first one did. That would explain the *decrease in productivity,* but with some additional training, they should recover quite quickly. I think *morale* has remained high because of good and consistent leadership characteristics, and that fact alone should make the adjustments easier for them.

"How did I do with my guesses, Liz?"

"You must be a wizard, Dr. Bankston. You were right on target with everything you said. Now that you are on a roll, want to join our team to help us tackle a few other medical offices, and the hospital upgrade?"

"I am afraid you may be right about needing help, Liz, but to answer your original question, I may not be the best one to help in your situation. I think, however, that I may be able to interest my colleague in that project. Her index, administered before a new change initiative, can track the emergence of symptoms and help you understand how to head off potential problems before they happen. How does that sound, Liz?"

"Like an answer to my prayers!"

Dr. Bankston smiled and said, addressing the group, "Now I want to say something more to you all in general. Each of you seem to have a good sense of where your company should be headed, and your instincts will only be enhanced as you put into practice what we've learned together. Because of your positions, I think understanding the potential impact of attachment behavior on your organization will serve you well. Please avail yourself of the opportunity to learn more about this subject and how it can assist you and your organization. You are all on the threshold of events that can have profound effects—either positive or negative. But by design or default, the pieces of the puzzle are now in your hands. Solve the puzzle by placing the pieces carefully, and the future is yours."

Brunch—10:30 a.m.

Dr. Bankston then turned toward Joe, who was still sitting across the room. "Joe, I see you over there; gotten any news yet?"

"Yes, sir; some good news too, I trust. First, the airport is supposed to be open for departures beginning about two o'clock. The roads are mostly clear, and I'll have the hotel van ready to take you there as soon as you're ready. That means you have about an hour or so to eat, if you are hungry. Second thing: just this minute I got the message that brunch is ready, and everyone is waiting for you in the breakfast room.

"One other thing, sir, if I may say something else. I told you my little girl left her cloth doll, Patty, at home, and she hasn't acted right since she got here. In fact, she's been behaving about the same way you say folks in your company have been behaving. Cranky, moping around, won't play with anything else, things like that. I couldn't help but overhear some of what you all were talking about, and I think you've shown me that she is just missing her Patty doll. It's funny to think that when a company changes something—and we're not talking about dolls and teddy bears here—that even the company leaders miss the things that they are used to having around, just like little folks do, too."

"Hmmmm. Did you hear that, group? It sounds like Joe pretty well summed it up for us. Do you think that may give us a theme for what we have tried to accomplish here, and its significance in why we act the way we do? Perhaps we should give more careful consideration to the importance of our transitional objects in the workplace whenever change is anticipated. And that reminds me of those little packages that I put out for you …"

Dr. Bankston was immediately met with a chorus of, "Oh yeah, what about these things?" "What should we do with them?" "Should we open them?"

"I hate to disappoint you, but they were actually empty when they were placed on the table Saturday morning. But now that you have had them with you for the past twenty-four hours or so … are they empty still? They may be a little battered by now, but I think that for at least a few of us, they have become a transitional object of sorts—representing some kind of stability and consistency during a topsy-turvy weekend.

"I hope they have convinced you that objects are not meaningful in and of themselves, but become meaningful because we choose to bestow meaning upon them. And in times of instability, the ones who adjust to change the best are the ones who can shift meaning easily from one object to another. Perhaps these little charm boxes can symbolize whatever we have accomplished here, and for each of us that will be something different. A bridge, perhaps, between something lost and something found.

"For me, this little box has become a symbol of all of those things that I have leaned on for security in the past, and which I will look for to lean on in the future. I'm going to put it up on the shelf beside my old 'Betsy.'

"At any rate, they do seem to now have more meaning than they did when I gave them out. They were just intended to distract you from the hurricane …"

The group looked at each other, and in unison replied, "What hurricane?" and the room filled with laughter.

The Science
behind the Story:
Understanding
Attachment

L ike Dr. Bankston and his colleagues, the mystery we all
face in the workplace is why, despite all our efforts and
experience in trying to manage change well, has the
change initiative failure rate remained at such a high level for
over twenty years? Why have our best efforts yielded so little
fruit?

Dr. Bankston believed that the answer could be found
in the *individual's* response to change. Indeed, not one of the
organizational change models presented for more than twenty
years has addressed this problem from the symptomatic
perspective of the individual employee. He had to go outside
his field for more evidence, and, perhaps to his surprise,

he found himself in the field of psychology—specifically, attachment theory. Here he found an explanation for the consistent reactions he saw in individuals experiencing change in the workplace; they seemed to be related to attachment theory and the symptoms typical of losing access to significant attachment objects.

Dr. Bankston's group seemed convinced of his theory. But were you convinced? Before you decide, it might help if you could learn more about the primary sources Dr. Bankston referenced, and hear how we, the authors, pieced them together ourselves.

General Principles

Since Kurt Lewin's groundbreaking work in 1951, multiple models to aid the process of organizational change have emerged. But why are all these well-researched and carefully crafted methodologies so often ineffective? Finally a few people have begun to notice that organizations really aren't addressing the internal natures of their employees that are—quite frankly—the source of common reactions to change in the workplace. For example, business professor and consultant Mitchell Marks (2010) has noted that "employees are more likely to hang on to the fear, uncertainty, resentment, and other emotions that big changes bring if it seems to them that management has no clue about how they feel. Leaders who acknowledge those feelings and help employees deal with them create an environment of cooperation and trust.". And consultant and leadership coach A.J. Schuler (2003) has said, "To win people's commitment for change, you must engage them on both a rational level and an emotional level ... in my experience it is the [impact of emotions] that 'would-be' change agents understand least well." The importance of these emotional reactions is surfacing in neuroscience research that will add new knowledge to the fields of leadership and management.

In fact, Jerry Harvey, professor emeritus at The George Washington University and author of *The Abilene Paradox* (1988), has pointed out that the problem may be in the term "resistance to change" itself. This term, commonly used by organizational change models as a common diagnosis for change initiative failure, implies that the employee is to blame, when the problem is more often the organization's failure to understand what is actually a natural human reaction to change. According to Harvey, employees aren't resisting change itself, but more specifically the sense of loss associated with the change (1999). If this is true, the more conventional change methodologies focus on solving the problem of "resistance to change" and the more they try to impose a solution, the more they miss the mark. In other words, perhaps the problem isn't that certain individuals are acting out of the ordinary when they resist organizational change—perhaps it's that we don't understand how natural it really is.

As we explained in the introduction, this mystery of why organizational change initiatives remain so prone to failure has plagued us for some time. When we initially discovered that psychological researcher Rene Spitz's work described, in very precise terms, the same reactions we were seeing in employees in virtually every organizational change situation, we couldn't help but wonder if there was a systematic connection.

Exhibit 1. Rene Spitz and the Symptoms of Loss

Just after World War II, Rene Spitz undertook a series of studies on disadvantaged infants in Romania (Spitz 1945;

1946; Spitz and Wolf 1946). In particular, he studied infants who had experienced inadequate mothering, separation, and depression. As a result of a series of articles he published on infant development, adoption procedures around the world were eventually changed, promoting a movement toward early adoption whenever feasible (Emde 1983, 4).

Whenever an infant's primary caregiver was changed, Spitz noticed that the infant would develop a consistent set of symptoms he termed "anaclitic depression." The term "anaclitic" derives from the Greek word *anaclisis,* which means "to lean on." In general terms, these symptoms were apprehension (anxiety), retardation of development, frustration, rejection of environment, refusal to participate, and withdrawal. In essence, then, anaclitic depression was a depressive state, or a period of instability, that inevitably occurred after the infant lost contact with his or her "love object," which, in this case, was the primary caregiver (Harvey 1999). Although first described in infants, these symptoms have also been found to develop in adults when the adult experiences a significant loss (Grady 2005).

Spitz's work was enough to get us thinking: Since these symptoms also occur in adults, might these symptoms also develop in the workplace, albeit in a somewhat altered form, when groups of individuals experience organizational change? To explore these connections and better define how organizational change impacts the employee in the workplace, I (VMG) began to develop a model describing the sequence of behaviors (or symptoms) that emerge during an organizational change initiative and their subsequent impact on the organization. This would become the Model of an Organizational Loss of Effectiveness (LOE).

Figure 2: Model of an Organizational LOE

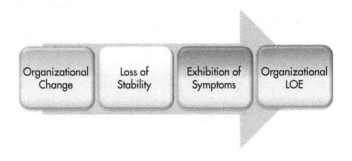

According to this research, organizational change causes a loss of stability that results in a predictable and measurable set of symptoms that closely resembles Spitz's symptoms of loss. Based on connections established by reviewing existing management literature and validated by the consent of a subject matter expert committee, we determined that the six relevant individual symptoms of Spitz corresponded to equivalent organizational symptoms. And when a sufficient number and/or intensity of these symptoms are present simultaneously, an organizational loss of effectiveness will occur (Grady 2005).

Table 1 shows how each individual symptom of loss translates into an organizational equivalent. (See Appendix B for a full explanation of how each individual symptom results in its organizational equivalent.)

Table 1: Individual Symptoms of Loss and Their Organizational Equivalents

Individual Symptoms ➡	Organizational Equivalents
Apprehension (Anxiety)	Decreased Morale
Frustration	Decreased Productivity
Retardation of Development	Decreased Motivation
Rejection of the Environment	Increased Conflict
Refusal to Participate	Increased Absenteeism
Withdrawal	Increased Turnover

While Spitz's work was groundbreaking in its significance, his work was never carried out to its full conclusion, so this evidence wasn't expansive enough to be convincing on its own. We wanted confirmation that these symptoms were not an anomaly, that they did exist, and that they were the result of the loss of something that had previously been "leaned on" or had been "depended upon" for stability. That's when we turned to the work of John Bowlby.

Exhibit 2. John Bowlby and Attachment Theory

John Bowlby is considered by many to be the father of attachment theory, and we found his work particularly relevant for several reasons: his work confirms the work of Spitz, his work spans several decades, and his work is very well known both inside and outside the field of psychology. Also, while most of Bowlby's work pertained to infants and children, he made two important additional points. First, he emphasized that attachment behavior is active into adulthood and throughout life, and second, its method of expression in adults may differ from that in children.

Just like Spitz and Wolf(1946), Bowlby also found that infants react strongly when they are separated from their mothers. This statement may be painfully obvious to anyone who spends time with infants, but the significance of Bowlby's work relates to *why* this strong reaction occurs. The major difference from Spitz is that Bowlby saw this reaction as *instinctual* rather than *depressive*. In Bowlby's words, "Attachment behavior is the result of the activity of behavioral systems that have a continuing set goal, that of maintaining a specified relationship [with the defined object]" (1969). In other words, this reaction is natural and healthy, rather than deviant or unhealthy.

Most of Bowlby's findings focused on studying the reaction of children who were temporarily separated from their mothers, and for which he is best known. But he was quick to recognize that attachment behavior persisted into and throughout adulthood, although in a somewhat altered or matured form. Bowlby established that adults tend to exhibit attachment behaviors primarily to remain in relationship to a spouse as well as to a group. In fact, attachment behaviors likely developed as a natural part of our species' survival strategy, since banding together in groups significantly enhanced the safety and survival of the groups' members.

Even beyond attachments to specific individuals and the family group or clan, Bowlby also recognizes and significantly expands the definition of attachment behavior. "While attachment behavior may change somewhat from infancy to childhood ... it remains a dominant strand in his life .... During adolescence and adult life attachment behavior is commonly directed to groups and organizations ... other than the family. A school, a college, a work group, a religious group, or a political group can come to constitute ... an attachment figure ... and is a straightforward continuation [in a more sophisticated form] of attachment behavior ... [throughout life] no form of behavior is accompanied by stronger feelings (emotions) than is attachment behavior" (Bowlby 1969, 207–209). Other possible attachment figures include objects such as a "familiar place, or social role" (1980, 245–246).

In other words, humans have always needed to find attachments in order to feel secure. It is only the nature of the objects to which we attach that has changed over time.

Connecting the Work of Spitz and Bowlby

To directly compare the findings of Spitz and Bowlby, we first examined Spitz's writings for his more explicit descriptions of anaclitic depression. We found he had observed the following behaviors in reaction to loss: "frustration, apprehension, sadness, weepiness; lack of contact, rejection of environment, withdrawal; retardation of development, retardation of reaction to stimuli, slowness of movement, dejection, stupor; loss of appetite, refusal to eat, loss of weight; insomnia." And elsewhere loss was characterized by "sadness and weeping ... withdrawal, loss of appetite, loss of interest in the outside world, dejection, retarded [development]" (Spitz and Wolf 1946, 316, 338). These behaviors are consistent with the "symptoms" referenced previously.

Similarly, Bowlby lists the following attachment behaviors resulting from separation and/or loss: "... protest ... despair ... detached ..." (1973, 26). Elsewhere, he also lists "agitation ..., crying, rejection of comforting gestures, and anxiety at a level that may lead to panic ... lethargy ... reductions in the level of activity, and altered sleeping and eating behavior… detached …" (Ziefman and Hazan 2008, 443), and "… numbness, yearning and protest, disorganization and despair" (Bretherton 1992, 13).

If we compare Spitz's symptoms with Bowlby's attachment behaviors, it is easy to imagine that they are describing the same condition. If there are differences, they seem to exist only in the matter of degree.

And comparing the symptoms side by side with the observed organizational responses, it seems even more likely that they are generally if not specifically equivalent, particularly after our experience observing the typical instabilities that employees experience after any kind of organizational change. We became convinced that whether we call these reactions to organizational change initiatives "symptoms" that result from anaclitic depression or "behaviors" activated by attachment issues, these behaviorial clusters that arise as a result of "loss" are equivalent, such that either cluster would similarly impact the integrity of the organization. See Table 2 below.

Table 2: Comparison of Symptoms

Individual Symptoms →	Organizational Equivalents ←	Activation of Attachment Behavior
Anxiety/ Apprehension	Decreased Morale	Anxiety/Distress Despair/ Hopelessness
Frustration	Decreased Productivity	
Retarded Development	Decreased Motivation	Agitation Numbness/ Yearning
Rejection of Environment	Increased Conflict	Protest/Anger
Refusal to Participate	Increased Absenteeism	Refusing comfort/ Denial
Withdrawal	Increased Turnover	Detachment

Reacting to change is an inherent part of our nature, and whether the resulting reactions are described as behaviors or symptoms may ultimately just be a matter of semantics. Out of respect to the two authors, for the most part we've found ourselves using the terms interchangeably. However, out of respect to the conventions of the medical field, when referring to them in the context of diagnosis and treatment, we've found it more convenient to use the terms associated with symptoms (as in Table 3 in the next section).

"We form attachment to objects unique to our organizational environment and we 'lean on' them for support."

Exhibit 3. D.W. Winnicott and Transitional Objects

The contributions mentioned above gave us most of the information we needed, but there were connecting pieces that were still missing (Grady and Grady, 2008). Spitz and Bowlby's research clearly had to do with our tendency to attach to *people* as a source of stability. And although Bowlby did extend the definition of attachment behaviors to groups themselves rather than merely individuals in the groups, Bowlby, for the most part, does not directly say whether or not healthy attachment figures can be inanimate objects, or even abstract objects such as a computer software program. What little he has to say on the matter is cryptic and in the context of D.W. Winnicott's work: "[A] way of looking at the role of these inanimate objects is to regard them simply as objects towards which certain components of attachment behavior come to be directed or redirected because the 'natural' object is unavailable" (Bowlby 1969, 312).

Winnicott, on the other hand, had plenty to say about attachment and inanimate objects. In 1951, he introduced the concept of transitional objects as a means to support individuals during transition or change. Winnicott's discussion highlights the unique and individualized nature of the transitional object. Children often attach to a transitional object, like a "binky" or a blanket or a doll, to replace their preferred constant contact with Mom. The attachment formed with the transitional object can also become quite intense, and just like Joe's daughter Marie found Raggedy Ann to replace her "Patty," so any object may temporarily serve to provide the illusion of support when our preferred objects are not available or have been changed.

This also applies to adults. Whether unconsciously or consciously, we form attachments to objects unique to our organizational environment that we "lean on" for support. When these attachment objects are removed or changed (i.e., a new technology is implemented, the organization is restructured, or a business process is reestablished). As a result we will experience and must deal with the grief that results from our feelings of loss. Winnicott (1971, 4) puts it even more strongly: "[transitional objects and transitional phenomena] … become vitally important [as] a defense against anxiety, especially anxiety of the depressive type." In other words, if we can't transition quickly enough to another transitional object, we'll become withdrawn, anxious, and depressed. These exact terms are very similar to those previously described in the findings of Spitz and Bowlby.

Reviewing the Evidence: Human Nature and Organizational Change Theory

So let's review the evidence. We know that organizational change can be challenging. We have discovered that although many well-established organizational change methodologies explain some parts of the change process well, used alone they meet with limited success. From Spitz and Bowlby, we've learned that human beings *instinctively* and often *subconsciously* attach to people, groups, or other objects to establish a sense of security throughout their lifetime, although adult attachment behaviors look different than children's. We've identified research-based behavioral symptoms that can emerge in the individual employee and whose collective impact (organizational equivalents) can reduce the effectiveness of the organization. And from Bowlby and Winnicott, we have learned that adults can attach to inanimate objects as well as to people or groups, and if our attachment objects are lost, we can also attach to other transitional objects to reestablish a sense of security.

Therefore, putting together the evidence we've seen from Spitz, Bowlby, and Winnicott, we'd like to propose a new definition of attachment behavior that takes into account the work of all three. Attachment behavior is the result of an internal response to any change that occurs outside one's self and that is perceived, either knowingly or unknowingly, as a "loss.". Attachment is an inherent part of human nature that provides us with a needed sense of security, and it interacts, usually unconsciously, with our environment. This, of course, includes our work environment. In this context, Harvey's point about why "resistance to change" (1999) is a misleading term makes even more sense: the essence of the problem is not resisting change per se, but resisting the *distress* inherent in losing objects we are *attached to* or *lean on* for support in our work environment. These objects can be people, systems, places, things, or even abstract concepts such as ideas or environments—anything that provides us with a sense of "attachment" to the organization.

In our view, Spitz, Bowlby, and Winnicott have provided the evidence needed to solve the mystery of why the change initiative failure rate is so high. Individuals aren't consciously resisting change because they are trying to be difficult; they're reacting quite naturally to the loss of an attachment. Certainly failing to account for basic human instinct could help explain this consistently high failure rate for organizational change initiatives.

But although understanding why people react to change the way they do is valuable in and of itself, understanding the true cause of our reaction also makes it much more likely we'll find an effective solution. In fact, attachment theory already suggests a solution that we as individuals know well and apply in other contexts: we just haven't realized it also applies to the workplace. Perhaps it is because no one has integrated the attachment aspect of human nature in the context of workplace change. We will address this in the next section.

Pivot to Success: Recognize, Support, Evaluate, Optimize

I f attachment is an inherent part of human nature, then our challenge as executives, managers, supervisors, and employees in any organizational change is to identify those attachments and how the impending change affects them, and try to design a solution. Success in organizational change depends upon maintaining healthy attachments, while supporting and facilitating the successful implementation of new technology, new business process, new systems, new leadership, new office space, and all other types of organizational change. This is what we have come to call *The Pivot Point* of organizational change success: when we recognize the significance of our individual reaction to organizational change, take appropriate steps to support healthy attachment behaviors, and make use of current information to optimize the situation for all concerned.

If Spitz, Bowlby, and Winnicott are right, then no matter how independent we may be or what position we hold, if we are human, we are *all* attached to objects. Remember, these objects can be tangible or intangible: people, systems, places, things, or ideas. Let's look at ourselves and see what we can admit about our own attachments. Which of the following are you attached to in *your* workplace? (Go ahead—write in the margins if you want to!)

- Your leadership role
- A software program
- Your office configuration: three walls and an open door
- Your phone system that makes communication possible
- The computer that sits on your desk
- The morning financial performance report
- The integrated resource system that lets you track manufacturing productivity at ten different locations
- The hardcopy medical record that is the trusted source of information and patient medical history
- The mp3 player that provides the day to day rhythm of the organization
- Support and encouragement from leadership
- The enterprise network system that lets you communicate with your colleagues in five different countries
- The reporting relationship between the management team and the employees
- The subway system that gets you to and from work each day

- The building break room or coffee kiosk that allows you to socialize with colleagues
- The organizational culture that fosters creativity and innovation
- The organizational structure that provides recognition, praise, and accolade for completed tasks
- Your job ... and that your job, as you know it, will exist tomorrow ....

"Success in organizational change depends upon maintaining healthy attachments."

We rely on external objects, like those listed above, for the predictability and security they inherently represent. We are instinctually driven throughout our lives to form these types of attachments, and we resent having them taken away from us. Now, as self-reliant adults, we may not like to hear this. But these patterns of attachment behavior are consistent with our human nature and verified by the Model of the Organizational LOE described above. Even the suggestion of removing a leaned-on object, not to mention the change itself, can create instability in individuals that can eventually bring the organization into an organizational LOE. This instinctive reaction is always present, no matter how much we consciously understand that an organizational change is needed objectively.

So to mitigate the negative effects of losing our sense of stability, one way an organization can ease the transition of a change initiative is to look for a generic substitute to replace the lost object until a new sense of stability is restored. The right (i.e., effective) transitional object for each employee will ultimately be unique; however, interim support should arise out of the culture of the organization, or department within the organization, and resonate with the individuals' nature, the organization, and the change project itself.

A replacement transitional object could be a leader, a favored object, a method of communication, a continuing education series, a physical space, a technology, a colleague, a culture, or any combination of these items. It can even differ from one change event to another. The transitional objects only have to provide a support system to the individual employees experiencing the organizational change. If successful, these new objects can serve as an interim point of stability during the potential disruption brought about by organizational change, and possibly provide support indefinitely.

In addition to the use of transitional objects, the Model of an Organizational LOE has shown us that symptoms may be prevented or modified before or even as they develop. Using qualitative interviews and/or a quantitative tool, an organization can discover which symptoms are most likely to escalate, allowing them to implement a strategy to mitigate these symptoms before they ever begin their organizational change initiative.

The qualitative approach begins with any trained change professionals conducting a series of employee interviews with subjective questions to predict those behaviors, perceptions, and attitudes likely to emerge in the individual in response to a change (see Table 3). Then internal change agents or external consultants can use these results to track the employee reactions to the change process. The most significant challenge to the qualitative process is insuring reliability and consistency of the subjective responses from the individual.

A quantitative method, on the other hand, is a more objective way to identify and measure the symptoms in question, and is usually more cost effective. The Change Diagnostic Index (see Appendix A) is one such instrument. This is a validated measurement tool (Grady, Gleckel, Grody, 2009 & Thomas, 2015) now available to organizations to help them measure the intensity of the six symptoms associated with new change initiatives. Employees impacted by the change complete a questionnaire anonymously, and measurements taken from employees' responses are grouped into demographic units as determined by the organization's leadership. This provides measurable data to observe, track, and evaluate the specific symptoms as they emerge in individuals during the implementation of a change initiative.

Based on our work with the Organizational LOE, we recommend a cumulative methodology that utilizes both limited qualitative interviews and the quantitative tool as the most efficient means to maximize change project success.

We suggest determining the intensity of symptoms *prior* to introducing the change. Often an organization would use a quantitative tool early in the planning process to predetermine what areas may be at most risk, allowing for any necessary risk management prior to the change. The results of the tool are then validated against the qualitative interviews to create a customized change strategy. Once the change is implemented, the survey is administered again to determine how the intensity of the various symptoms has changed. After this assessment, the organization could initiate the appropriate mitigation and intervention strategies to ease the corresponding elevated symptoms.

This measureable data enables the organization to identify symptoms, provide information, and identify the most appropriate and timely intervention for that *unique* organization. Integrating the quantitative tool with the qualitative interviews simply provides a more comprehensive and proactive organizational change process. In addition to valuable insights that is otherwise unachievable in the change process.

Table 3, on the next page, offers some suggested interventions for particular symptoms to provide a starting point for organizations to reduce the intensity of symptoms resulting from an organizational change initiative. You can read more about these intervention strategies in Appendix B.

These suggested mitigation or intervention strategies have worked consistently for other organizations experiencing the corresponding symptoms. It's not that these strategies are new or unique; the existing change literature recognizes each one. But what is unique, and what might explain the lack of success in purely organizational approaches, is the incredible value of correlating the emerging symptoms and creating a customized and comprehensive change plan focused on the individual as the core component, and then crafting a solution appropriately considering the needs of all concerned.

At last count, we had used this index in a number approaching ten thousand employees in a variety or organizations from large to small, including the federal government, health care organizations, higher and secondary education, nonprofits, and business and industry. In each organization, we have repeatedly heard comments like "Thank you for listening to us," "Thank you for helping me to understand myself," and "Thank goodness this wasn't just another survey; this one was actually useful—very much so." These comments come not just from top leadership or management, who might be justifiably satisfied at solving difficult change management problems, but from front-line workers, some of whom felt for the first time that someone finally heard and actually acted on those issues affecting them.

In light of the success we've seen with this approach, we suggest that symptom assessment become an integral component of a more comprehensive change methodology, in order to truly maximize the success potential of the change initiative and give every organization the opportunity to reach its Pivot Point.

Conclusion

So, what do you think? Has the mystery of the persistently high failure rate for organizational change initiative been solved? Even if the evidence seems logical, the only way to know for sure is to test it out in the field. As for us, we will keep on

Table 3: Symptoms + Mitigation Strategy

Individual Symptoms (Bowlby equivalents)	Organizational Symptoms	Suggested Mitigation/ Intervention Strategy
Anxiety (Anxiety/ Distress, Despair/ Hopelessness)	**Decreased Morale**	**Enhance and Increase Support from Leadership/ Sponsorship**
Frustration (Agitation)	**Decreased Productivity**	**Increase Education/ Training with the Identified Change**
Retardation of Development (Numbness/ Yearning)	**Decreased Motivation**	**Integrate Individual Coaching**
Rejection of the Environment (Protest/Anger)	**Increased Conflict**	**Improve Communication— Subordinate, Colleague, and Supervisor**
Refusal to Participate (Refusing Comfort/ Denial)	**Increased Absenteeism**	**Evaluate Employee Engagement and Support**
Withdrawal (Detachment)	**Increased Turnover**	**Monitor Job Satisfaction and Commitment**

testing and learning from each opportunity until the change implementation failure rate approaches zero.

But what about your organization? Why not try using some of what you have learned about this "attachment" theory during your next change initiative? See if it helps. Feel free to contact us at www.pivotpnt.com, and let us know your verdict.

And if you run across any other unsolved mysteries in the workplace, please let us know. Dr. Bankston and Company are always up for another challenge.

New Research

INTRODUCTION

Since the original publication date, new areas have been defined that are both material and substantial additions to the research related to workplace attachment behavior. One area includes learned behaviors that are related to the quality of attachment support a person received during the first few years of life. This type of learned behavior is referred to as an attachment style. Research in this area has turned out to be a valuable contribution to our work.

Another area has revealed a relationship between neuroscience research and attachment behavior. This is associated with a very primitive area of the brain that supports our survival needs. (Panksepp and Bevin, 2012) Related to this finding is an area associated with loss and the grief that follows any loss. However. when handled properly, this period of grief can lay the foundation for a period of personal and organizational growth. (Grady & Grady, 2017)

ATTACHMENT STYLES

The research on attachment styles is based on aspects of attachment behavior determined by the caring dynamics between the caregiver and the child during the child's first few years. The nature of this relationship determines the nature of an adult's attachment style. Based on two internal working models, each person develops either a positive or negative image of themselves, and also, either a positive or negative image for others. (Boatwright, et al., 2010)

Individuals can generally be defined as having one of four accepted attachment styles: Secure, Avoidant, Preoccupied, and Anxious. Each of these styles are described below.

- A person with a Secure attachment style is generally resilient and comfortable with change, but can often miss the impact of change on others. Examples include trust in leadership and a belief they can transition through the change.
- A person with an Avoidant attachment style tends to distance and disengage themselves from change initiatives because they have low expectations for others. Examples would be independent operators, people sensitive to rejection and those who seek positive personal achievements.
- A person with a Preoccupied attachment style emphasizes high connection to others in the workplace, but often exhibit stress in the face of change and seek validation. An example is the need for reassurance, greater need for leadership presence, anxiety in the face of change.

- A person with an Anxious attachment style can find change challenging because of difficulties with trust and dependence on others. An example is mistrust of those closest to them, and involves avoidance, suppression and withdrawal.

Understanding attachment styles will allow the leader to better understand him or herself and become more supportive of other employee styles. Based on the successful implementation of these principles, research with organizations is working to promote a more prominent understanding and use of relational style in their leadership. This improves the consistency of leader/worker relationship, worker satisfaction, loyalty and the predictability of employee behavior.

NEUROSCIENCE

As humans we perceive ourselves as individuals, yet we depend on relationships with others as we adjust to the world in which we live. Our lives are implicitly controlled by biological forces within us and the external forces in our environments. The input from our inner, or interpersonal, environment is captured by internal sympathetic and parasympathetic sensory sources. Data regarding the surrounding world is accumulated from external sensory sources related to scent, sight, taste, hearing, temperature, touch, and pain. Our initial reaction to any incoming internal and external data happens instantly, but takes at least a fraction of a second or longer before the received information is transferred to other areas of our brain for further processing. It is only then that our more learned and purposeful reactions are shaped.

There are several survival related feelings, or affects, categorized by Panksepp and Biven (2012). Probably the most important is the "seeking" affect. The infant usually seeks and finds security in the care of the mother. In adults, we seek and find security and companionship in groups. In more ancient times, as individuals we were vulnerable to predators, but by forming into coherent groups. we could not only survive attacks from predators, but also thrived from the other benefits of collaboration. Once a group is formed, certain efforts are required to maintain the integrity of the group. This comes in the form of cooperative or pleasurable behavior in the form of "caring" and "playing" games when free time is available. Non-pleasurable threats and unfortunate circumstances result in "panic/grieving" behavior. Fear is another unfortunate feeling that here is represented by hard-wired reaction to predators, snakes, spiders, and heights, and learned responses to other dangers. In order to survive we learn from both these pleasurable and not-pleasurable sources. (Panksepp and Bevin, 2012)

The sensations we receive from these affects (pleasurable and non-pleasurable) are "hard-wired" reactions supported by immediate and automatically reflex actions (e.g. fight or flight) that served our earliest ancestors and aided them in their survival. Although these feelings exist only at the edge of awareness, they still have a profound impact on our lives and the architecture of our brains.

This primitive desire for survival directly connects adults to attachments in the workplace; it is this drive to survive that supports our security by forming complex attachment systems to things we encounter where we live and where we work.

LOSS, GRIEF, AND GROWTH

The activation of this primitive panic/grief mechanism also has a secondary consideration that should be noted. After a loss, or a perceived loss, we enter into a grieving process; the intensity of the process is usually dependent on how intense the loss is to each person affected. After experiencing loss, we mourn and endure a period that seems disconnected from reality; it is as if life has lost all meaning. To recover we must be able replace once comfortable "old" habits or thoughts with new and more unfamiliar and uncomfortable ones. This is the process of re-adjusting to a new reality. If an organizational loss is understood and supported by management, the grieving period can be shortened, and can also lead to improvements. Bowlby (1980) has stated that the mentally healthy person can emerge from loss " … with behavior, thoughts, and feelings reorganized … " (p. 245) factors that encourage and facilitate personal and organizational growth.

For more information on the material presented in the Addendum, and also other topics in this book, a deeper discussion can be found in the more recent book by Grady, Grady, et al. (2020).

Appendix A
The Change Diagnostic Index

The Change Diagnostic Index, originally known as the LOE Index, is a quantitative individual assessment tool based on the Model of an Organizational LOE. This index focuses on the nature and intensity of the six primary symptoms that develop in individual employees in response to a change initiative. The symptomatic responses are then related to the patterns of behaviors, perceptions, and attitudes that are the organizational manifestations of those symptoms as referenced in Table 1. The Change Diagnostic Index was designed to provide quantitative data that could be used to identify, monitor, and track emerging symptoms. This data/ information supports the agility organizations need in order to react and plan more efficiently dealing with the impact of the change.

The Change Diagnostic Index (CDI) was first referred to as the Loss of Effectiveness Index (LOE). The concept was designed and initially tested between 2005 and 2007 to measure six disruptive symptoms (see Appendix B) that often emerge as a result of organizational change. The CDI can be used to quantitatively measure and track the evidence of instability using either the 54 or 25 question version of the survey. These results can provide either a "snapshot" to assess an organization for internal areas of instability, or to provide a baseline for future comparison when tracking the progress of quality improvement efforts. The reiterative administration of the Change Diagnostic Index provides the organization with objective information to identify, measure, evaluate, and track the real-time results of an organizational change initiative.

Testing of the Change Diagnostic Index (2009) demonstrated high internal consistency and reliability for the assessment of loss of effectiveness. Internal consistency reliability testing resulted in a Cronbach's Alpha (Cronbach 1951) between 85 and 91 on all six domains in the Change Diagnostic Index. A test/retest of the index using Wilcoxon Signed Rank Test (Wilcoxon 1945) resulted in no significant difference between first test and second test. Content validity is demonstrated based on the development of the index from well-established constructs in the fields of employee morale and work preferences, anxiety, stress, frustration, and depression. Face validity was established through multiple reviews by experts in social psychology and organizational behavior (Grady, et al, 2009). The validity and reliability qualities were re-tested in 2015 and the previous results were reconfirmed. (Thomas, 2015)

Appendix B
Descriptions of Individual Symptoms, Their Organizational Equivalents, and Suggested Intervention Strategies

The specific terms outlined below and the definitions that we use associated with those terms evolved out of the descriptions of Spitz and Bowlby, and as much as possible are based on the classical meanings associated with those terms.

Apprehension (Anxiety) Leads to Loss of Morale

Anxiety is a state of chronic apprehension characterized by signs of tension and usually in reaction to some stressor. In organizations, a chronically anxious state results in a reduction in the morale within the organization. Morale is defined as the mental and emotional condition (enthusiasm, confidence, or loyalty) of an individual or group with regard to the function or tasks at hand, or as a sense of common purpose with respect to a group (*Merriam-Webster*). This is often the first sign of the loss of stability in an organization as a result of a change initiative.

Intervention: Enhance and Increase Support from Leadership. Anxiety/morale issues arising during a change initiative usually respond to support from leadership or sponsorship. Depending on the circumstances, this can be in the form of increased presence, gestures of support, increased interaction, etc. Support from the leadership reduces the perception of a threat and change-related stressors, which improves morale (Prosci* 2007; 2009).

Frustration Leads to Loss of Productivity

Individuals become frustrated when they are prevented from doing or achieving something (*Merriam-Webster*). As a result, they begin to lose interest, often become irritable, and may quit working on the project that is the cause of their frustration. As a result, their level of productivity declines. Productivity is defined as yielding results, benefits, or profits or devoted to the satisfaction of wants or the creation of utilities (*Merriam-Webster*). Frustration, and the corresponding loss of productivity, can often be a reaction to a lack of understanding of the reason or the nature of the change, or one's role in the process.

Intervention: Increase Education/Training. The loss of productivity resulting from frustration, often occurring during the adjustment period to a change event, can usually be effectively addressed through education and training (Magda 2009). Because frustration often results when an individual has difficulty completing tasks well, frustration improves when the individual receives assistance in functioning within the scope of change and can remain or become productive in light of the change.

Rejection of Environment Leads to Conflict

Rejection of the environment is usually a consequence of the individual "rejecting" some aspect of the new change initiative affecting their work environment, which they view as having been forced on them. The reaction leads to issues of conflict in the workplace directed at the change itself, directed at the supervisors seen as responsible for the change, or displaced onto co-workers. This conflict is the mental struggle resulting from incompatible or opposing needs, drives, wishes, or external or internal demands (*Merriam-Webster*).

Intervention: Improve Communication. Rejection of environment/conflict usually responds to increased or enhanced communication activities. Communication problems are often a "beneath the surface" sign of resenting the change. Areas for improvement include poor communication, tenuous work relationships, questionable managerial authority, or unclear chain of command (Fortado 2001), and bad information, lack of teamwork, or unclear work procedures/rules (Virovere, Kooskora, and Valler 2002).

Retardation of Development Leads to Lack of Motivation

The expression "retardation of development" implies that an individual has ceased to develop as a working component of the organization. This can be seen as a lack of motivation or impediment to the continuing development and skills of the affected employees of the organization (*Merriam-Webster*).

Organizational change can be a threat to competence, relatedness, and autonomy. When the threat to competence is sufficient in a group of employees, it results in a lessening level of motivation, and the result is work with less effort and attention to detail (Ryan and Deci 2000).

Intervention: Integrate Individual Coaching. Retardation of development usually responds to coaching focused on reviving their skills and showing individuals impacted by the change how it can work in their favor (Kotter 1998).

Refusal to Participate Leads to Absenteeism

One aspect of absence is, of course, not being present at work. Perhaps more importantly, it can also mean that the employees are lost in their own thoughts—daydreaming, planning a vacation, making unnecessary phone calls, and anything else that distracts them from issues at work—and for that reason, they are not being attentive (*Merriam-Webster*). There are two types of absenteeism relevant to organizational change and the loss of organizational effectiveness. The first is absence due to a change in job satisfaction, and the second is absence based on dysfunctional relations that have developed between the employee and employer (Nicholson and Johns 1985).

Intervention: Employee Engagement and Support. Refusal to participate/absenteeism is usually a result of a lack of adequate employee support and engagement. Engagement increases perceived value. A compromised employee, especially in a leadership or sponsorship role, can disrupt the entire change project (Prosci[*] 2007; 2009). Supporting employees by providing the opportunity and encouragement to become more involved and working to build commitment is one way to deal with this difficult problem.

Withdrawal Leads to Turnover

Employee withdrawal can be viewed as a "volitional response to perceived aversive conditions, designed to increase the physical and/or physiological distance between the employee and the organization" (Gupta and Jenkins 1982). Loss of stability created by the implementation of a new organizational change event can negatively impact employee job satisfaction and weaken the employees' commitment to the organization; these factors can contribute to increased turnover.

Intervention: Address Job Satisfaction and Commitment. Implement individual coaching to support, assess, and correct factors influencing job satisfaction and commitment. Turnover is generally preceded by consistent increase in at least four of the other symptoms. Therefore, it is not only the turnover that must be monitored and addressed, but also other symptoms.

Appendix C

The Colleague's E-mail to Dr. Bankston

To: <u>wbankston@bankstonandassociates.com</u>
Subject: RE: organizational change and attachment theory
Dear Dr. Bankston,

Thank you so much for your phone call—it was good to hear from you! Yes, as we discussed I have been working on this issue a lot, so feel free to share any of our conversation with your group. I have included below a synopsis of frequently asked questions that I think provide further explanation of what you've already been discussing. And forgive me if I get long-winded! I hope this helps and that your stormy weekend is a productive one …

Question: Why is Change So Hard?

The bottom line is that it is simply not in our nature to accept change. If we look far back into our history, or at primitive groups that still live in the shadows of our modern world, we will see that for most of human existence, change has presented a threat to our survival. As a result, there has developed within us a warning system, a sense of insecurity or instability, that has become associated with change.

Although organizational change in today's world is not often a threat to our survival, this is, however, a lingering perception that is deeply imbedded within our human natures. For that reason a change—for example, the threatened removal or replacement of something familiar—triggers the same reactions that may have once been implemented to improve our chances of survival. As a reaction to this change, certain behaviors arise that are designed to allow us to avoid or get rid of the things that we now perceive as a threat to the status quo, and that led to the feelings of instability.

The individual behaviors primarily aimed at avoiding the things associated with the change are:

> **Anxiety/Apprehension**
> **Frustration**
> **Retardation of Development**
> **Refusal to Participate**

The individual behaviors primarily aimed at removing the things associated with the change are:

> **Rejection of the environment**
> **Withdrawal**

Question: How are these behaviors expressed in an organization?

When a change initiative takes place in an organization, those affected by the change will experience a mixture of behaviors that themselves seem to be infectious and may spread to others that are not even directly involved in the change. The number and the intensity of the expression of these behaviors will be determined by the nature and culture of the organization and its supporting society. Here's a summary of the collective impact of the behaviors:

An increase in **"Anxiety/Apprehension"** will often dampen the **"Morale"** of those in the organization, and leads to worry and hopelessness.

Increased **"Frustration"** causes employees to become less effective and leads to decreases in **"Productivity"** within the organization, which may lead to haphazard and impatient attitudes.

"Retardation of Development" leads to a loss or lessening of the **"Motivation"** of those within the organization, which inhibits learning and applying effort to a task.

"Rejection of the Environment" leads to increases in the various forms of **"Conflict."** Anger, resentment, and hostility arise toward the change initiative, the organization, and each other.

A **"Refusal to Participate"** leads to various types of **"Absenteeism,"** not only being physically absent from work, but also being mentally distracted while at work, causing errors and mistakes.

"Withdrawal" leads to organizational **"Turnover."**

Question: Does this mean that these behaviors will have a negative impact on the organization?

The result, or the effect of whatever is going on in the employees' minds, consciously or unconsciously, has a progressive and collective impact on the entire organization. We have learned to express it in this sequence: Organizational change causes instability in the employees, which in turn leads to symptoms. When the number and/or intensity of the symptoms rise above a certain level, an organizational loss of effectiveness occurs. This is when productivity and profitability begins to decline— the negative impact has occurred.

It is the missing human component that is the "wild card" in the change process. The good news is that in most cases, being fairly adaptable beings, we will eventually accept a change initiative, but not without causing significant disruptions and distractions along the way. The major disruptions are related to decreases in productivity, absenteeism, and turnover, and the distractions come in the form of decreases in morale, motivation, and conflict.

Question: What can be done about change, and its impact on us and the organization collectively?

Most organizational change takes place in an effort to make the organization more effective and or efficient in some way, and to keep up with the competition. In the twenty-first century, frequent change is necessary for the survival of most organizations, but it comes with a price that has often been neglected. Because of our natures, people do not change very easily.

Over the past twenty years, there has been a great effort to develop effective change methodologies that organize and orchestrate the organizational change process. These are very important and necessary first steps, and many outstanding change process methods are now in place. However many studies over the past fifteen years have shown that 70 percent of organizational change initiatives fail at some level. This proves that while the mechanics of the change process may be tried and tested, this alone is insufficient—the human component is missing. They fail to see the impact of the change on the individual. That is the issue at hand: how do we integrate an understanding and acceptance of human nature into the workings and decisions that take place inside our organizations? We believe that this begins with something like the LOE Index, which was designed to identify and track the emergence of these behaviors, and try to intervene before they cause detrimental effects to the nature of the organization's efforts.

Hope this helps. Let me know if you need anything else. Best to Barbara and your family!

P.S. How's Betsy? VMG

References

Beer, Michael, and Nitin Nohria. 2000. *Breaking the Code of Change.* Boston: Harvard Business School Press.

Bennett, John L. 2001. "Change Happens." *HR Magazine* (September): 149–156.

Black, Sandra E., and Lisa M. Lynch. 1997. "How to Compete: The Impact of Workplace Practices and Information Technology on Productivity." *NBER Working Papers6120.* National Bureau of Economic Research, Inc.

Bliese, Paul D., and Thomas W. Britt. 2001. "Social Support, Group Consensus, and Stressor-Strain Relationships: Social Context Matters." *Journal of Organizational Behavior* 22: 425–436.

Boatwright, K., Lopez, F., Sauer, E., Van Der Wege, A., Huber, D. (2010). The influence of adult attachment styles on workers' preferences for relational leadership behaviours. The Psychologist-Manager Journal, 13: 1–14.

Bowlby, John. 1969. *Attachment and Loss, Vol. 1: Attachment.* New York: Basic Books.

Bowbly, John. 1973. *Attachment and Loss, Vol. 2: Separation.* New York: Basic Books.

Bowlby, John. 1980. *Attachment and Loss, Vol. 3: Loss.* New York: Basic Books.

Bowlby, John. 1988. *A Secure Base: Parent-Child Attachment and Healthy Human Development.* New York: Basic Books.

Bretherton, Inge. 1992. "The Origins of Attachment Theory: John Bowlby and Mary Ainsworth." *Developmental Psychology* 28: 759–775.

Celnar, Christine. 1999. "Personality and Justice Predictors of Workplace Resistance to Organizational Change." Master's thesis, University of Calgary.

Cronbach, Lee. 1951. "Coefficient Alpha and the Internal Structure of Tests." *Psychometrika* 16: 297–334.

Eisold, Ken. 2010. "Resistance to Change in Organizations." Hidden Motives blog. *Psychology Today.* http://www.psychologytoday.com/blog/hidden-motives/201005/resistance-change-in-organizations.

Emde, Robert. 1983. "Editor's Introduction to Deprivation of Mothering." In *Rene A. Spitz: Dialogues from Infancy: Selected Papers,* edited by Robert Emde, 3–4. New York: International Universities Press.

Fortado, Bruce. 2001. "The Metamorphosis of Workplace Conflict." *Human Relations* 24 (9):1189–2001.

Goodman, Paul S., and Robert S. Atkin. 1984. *Absenteeism: New Approaches to Understanding, Measuring, and Managing Employees' Absence.* San Francisco: Jossey-Bass.

Grady, Victoria M., and James D. Grady. 2011. "The Relationship of Bowlby's Attachment Theory to the Persistent Failure of Organizational Change Initiatives." Unpublished manuscript last modified November 9.

Grady, Victoria M, Beverly Magda, and James D. Grady. 2011. "Organizational Change, Mental Models, and Stability: Are They Mutually Exclusive or Inextricably Linked?" *Journal of Organizational Development* 29 (3) 9-22.

Grady, Victoria, and James Grady. 2011. "Organizational Mistrust: Exploring the Issue, Pondering the Fate…." *Journal of Organisational and Social Dynamics* 11 (1) 41-58.

Grady, V. & Grady, J. (2017). "Letting go" and "moving on": mourning and strategic capacity. In Osnes (Ed): Family capitalism: Best practices in ownership and leadership. London: Routledge Taylor Francis Group.

Grady, J., Grady, V., McCreesh, P., Noakes, I. (2020). Workplace attachments: Managing beneath the surface. New York: Routledge.

Grady, Victoria, Erica Gleckel, and Erin Grody. 2009. "Organizational Loss of Effectiveness (LOE) Model and the LOE Index: A Quantitative Measurement Tool for Identifying Individual Symptomatic Response to Technological Change." *Integration Journal*: 97–106.

Grady, Victoria and James Grady. 2008. "Winnicott's Potential Space and Transitional Objects: Implications for the Organizational Change Process and Its Previously Defined Relationship to an Organizational LOE." *Journal of Organizational and Social Dynamics* 8 (2): 278–297.

Grady, Victoria. 2005. "Studying the Effect of Loss of Stability on Organizational Behavior: A Perspective of Technological Change." PhD dissertation, The George Washington University.

Gupta, Nina and G. Douglas Jenkins. 1982. "Absenteeism and Turnover: Is There a Progression?" *Journal of Management Studies* 19: 395–412.

Harvey, Jerry. 1988. *The Abilene Paradox and Other Meditations on Management*. San Francisco: Jossey-Bass.

Harvey, Jerry. 1999. *How Come Every Time I Get Stabbed in the Back My Fingerprints Are on the Knife?* San Francisco: Jossey-Bass.

Harvard Business Review (HBR). 1998. *Harvard Business Review on Change*. Boston: Harvard Business Review Press.

Hom, Peter W., and Rodger W. Griffith. 1995. *Employee Turnover*. Cincinnati: South-Western.

IBM Institute for Business Value (IBM). 2008. "Making Change Work: Continuing the Enterprise of the Future Conversation." http://www-935.ibm.com/services/us/gbs/html/gbs-making-change-work.html. Retrieved November 2, 2009.

Kotter, John. 1995. "Leading Change: Why Transformation Efforts Fail." *Harvard Business Review* (March-April): 1–20.

Lewin, Kurt. 1951. *Field Theory in Social Science.* New York: Harper and Row.

Lynch, James. 1977. *The Broken Heart: The Medical Consequences of Loneliness.* New York: Basic Books.

Magda, Beverly. 2009. "Increasing the Efficacy of Emergency Departments through Systems Analysis of Enterprise Architecture: Mitigating the Impact of Technological Change. PhD dissertation The George Washington University.

Marks, Mitchell. 2010. "In with the New: Change Is Never Easy." *Wall Street Journal,* May 24.

Merriam-Webster Online Dictionary (Merriam-Webster). http://www.m-w.com.

Miller, Jeffrey A., 2003. "Calming the Anxious Organization." *Employment Relations Today* (Winter): 11–18.

Mobley, William H. 1977. "Intermediate Linkages in the Relationship between Job Satisfaction and Employee Turnover." *Journal of Applied Psychology* 62 (April): 237–240.

Nicholson, Nigel, and Gary Johns. 1985. "The Absence Culture and the Psychological Contract—Who's in Control of Absence?" *Academy of Management Review* 10 (3): 397–407.

Noer, David. 1993. *Healing the Wounds: Overcoming the Trauma of Layoffs and Revitalizing Downsized Organizations.* San Francisco: Jossey-Bass.

Panksepp, J., & Biven, L. (2012). The archaeology of mind: Neuroevolutionary origins of human emotions. New York, NY: W. W. Norton & Company.

Prosci*. 2007. *Best Practices in Change Management: Benchmarking Report.*

Prosci*. 2009. *Best Practices in Change Management: Benchmarking Report.*

Raps, Andreas. 2004. "Implementing Strategy." *Strategic Finance* (June): 49–53.

Ryan, Richard, and Edward Deci. 2000. "Self-Determination Theory and the Facilitation of Intrinsic Motivation, Social Development, and Well-Being." *American Psychological Association* 55 (1): 68–78.

Schuler, A.J. 2003. "Overcoming Resistance to Change: Top Ten Reasons for Change Resistance." Schuler Solutions. http://www.schulersolutions.com/resistance_to_change.html.

Senge, Peter. 1999. *The Dance of Change: The Challenges to Sustainng Momentum in Learning Organizations.* New York: Doubleday.

Spitz, Rene. 1945. *The Psychoanalytic Study of the Child, Vol. 1.* New York: International Universities Press.

Spitz, Rene. 1946. *The Psychoanalytic Study of the Child, Vol. 2.* New York: International Universities Press.

Spitz, Rene, and Katherine Wolf. 1946. "Anaclitic Depression: An Inquiry into the Genesis of Psychiatric Conditions in Early Childhood, II." In Spitz, *The Psychoanalytic Study of the Child, Vol. 2*, 313–342.

Standish Group International. 2009. CHAOS Summary 2009. http://www.standishgroup.com/newsroom/chaos_2009.php. Retrieved November 1, 2009.

Standish Group Chaos Report (2015). Retrieved February 16, 2020. https://www.standishgroup.com/sample_research_files/CHAOSReport2015-Final.pdf

Strebel, Paul. 1998. "Why Do Employees Resist Change?" *Harvard Business Review on Change*, 139–157.

Thomas, A. J. (2015) Stat Consulting, unpublished work.

Virovere, Anu, Mari Kooskora, and Martin Valler. 2002. "Conflict as a Tool for Measuring Ethics at Workplace." *Journal of Business Ethics* 39 (August): 75–81.

Wilcoxon, Frank. 1945. "Individual Comparisons by Ranking Methods." *Biometrics Bulletin* 1 (6):80–83.

Winnicott, D. W. 1971. *Playing and Reality.* New York: Basic Books.

Ziefman, Debra, and Cindy Hazan. 2008. "Pair Bonds as Attachments." In J. Cassidy and P. Shaver, *Handbook of Attachment, 2nd. ed.*, 436-455. New York: Guilford Press.

Acknowledgments

From James

I must first acknowledge the assistance of those mentors who were unaware of their efforts in behalf of my education. There has been the Holy Bible, which has given me much more material to ponder than I would ever be able to fully explore. There have also been many writers, such as M. Scott Peck, Joseph Campbell, Robert A. Johnson, and Carl G. Jung, who have kept my imagery growing. And then there are those who have written in a more popular vein, who may have set out only to write a book, but instead have added to the new mythologies that nurture our souls when we didn't even know that our souls needed nurturing: George Lucas (the *Star Wars* series, especially *Episode IV*), J.R.R. Tolkien (*The Lord of the Rings* series), and J.K. Rowling (the *Harry Potter* series).

Then I must acknowledge the assistance of those who may have directly, if unwittingly, assisted me with inspiration, encouragement, and motivation to look further than I could have ever looked or even thought to look on my own, and who have played a bigger role in this book than they could ever know: Dr. Elliott Jaques (1917-2003) and Dr. Jerry Harvey.

I also wish to acknowledge my loyal and dedicated employees, who always accepted me just as I was, and those patient patients, all of whom have provided me with educational experiences and material, and with the inspiration and the excuse to dig a little deeper in my effort to understand the nature of their behaviors just a bit better than I had before.

There were some aspects of preparing this manuscript for publication that required certain skills that were beyond our capability. In this regard, to John McNutt for his skill in putting together the graphics displays, to Amanda Rooker for her editing expertise and advice, and to the capable and supportive staff of Morgan James Publishing I would like to express our most sincere appreciation.

Finally, I wish to acknowledge the assistance of my family and friends, and especially Anne, my wife of over 45 years. All of you and especially you, for helping when you felt you could help, for being there when being there was enough, and sometimes for just giving me space when I needed to walk alone.

Thank you all. —**JDG**

From Victoria

Thank you to Dr. Jerry Harvey, who in the beginning, challenged me to "learn" to write and later introduced me to concepts that have and will forever influence my unique worldview. To my husband, David F McCallum and my precious little girls, Kendall and Reagan, thank you for your incredible patience as

The Pivot Point was "translated" from an abstract concept deep in my mind into a readable format that can be shared.

To the thousands of individuals over the past 15 years that have been willing to share (or lament about) countless stories (and challenges) of organizational change experiences that served to validate and further substantiate the role of attachment in organizational behavior. Without corroboration, this would have likely remained an abstract concept relegated solely to academic literature.

Finally, thank you to my friends and family who supported and encouraged me, especially my Mimi, who through our unique experience, never let me forget that we were all equal, it is what you do with that equality that will ultimately set you apart. —**Victoria**

About the Authors

Dr. Victoria Grady (Jr.) completed her doctoral studies at The George Washington University in May 2005. Her dissertation focused on the inherent loss of stability suffered by organizations introducing and implementing organizational change initiatives. The research resulted in a validated model (<u>Change Diagnostic Index</u>) explaining the tendency of individuals, often subconsciously, to struggle, resist, and potentially disrupt the organizational change initiative.

Dr. Grady continues to build upon her research in the field of of change management and extended her original model to include a validated index (<u>Change Diagnostic Index</u>) that quantitatively measures the tendency of individuals within the organization to embrace organizational change initiatives. The index focuses on the employee and how factors inherent in organizational change impact their performance and profitability and subsequently have a negative impact on the overall health of the organization.

She is currently Director of the Master of Science in Management Program and an Associate Professor of Organizational Behavior in the School of Business at George Mason University. Dr. Grady's consulting practice includes federal government institutions, nonprofit organizations, and private sector companies. For more information, please contact her at vmgrady@pivotpnt.com or visit her website at www.pivotpnt.com

Dr. James Grady (Sr.) received his DMD at the University of Alabama, Birmingham, in 1971, and his residency training and a Master of Science in Oral and Maxillofacial Surgery at the University of North Carolina at Chapel Hill in 1974. He received a Master of Science in Psychology with a specialty in Organizational Psychology from Capella University in 2019. Dr. Grady was the Founder and Managing Partner at Oral and Maxillofacial Surgery of East Alabama from 1976 to 2009.

In his practice and as an avocation, he has been a keen observer and student of behavior. This has given him the opportunity to accumulate clinical knowledge regarding the various circles of cause and effect in chronic pain patients and in employees and colleagues, especially when under various types of stress. These interests have led him on what he describes as a fascinating journey of discovery both in his field and in the field of management in general. Prior to selling his practice in 2009, he served as a principal presenter at practice management workshops entitled "Enhancing Productivity" and "Conflict Management" at the American Association of Oral and Maxillofacial Surgeons Annual Meetings in 1995, 1996, and 1997, and "Office Management for the OMS Practice" in 1998.

Dr. Grady currently resides in Alabama, where he continues to practice oral surgery on a limited basis. He has been an active participant in the development of the LOE Index and continues to aggressively pursue a more comprehensive understanding of the intersection of human nature and organizational behavior. He presently serves as a consultant in health care, educational, and business-related sectors. For more information, please contact him directly at jdgrady@pivotpnt.com or visit his website at www.pivotpnt.com.

Printed in the USA
CPSIA information can be obtained
at www.ICGtesting.com
JSHW082214140824
68134JS00014B/618

9 781614 483007